VILLAGE LIFE AND LABOUR

T0352089

VILLAGE LIFE AND LABOUR

AN ANTHOLOGY

Selected and Edited

by

CECIL G. HUTCHINSON
Senior English Master, The Grammar School, Audenshaw

and

FRANK CHAPMAN
English Master, The Grammar School, Audenshaw

CAMBRIDGE
AT THE UNIVERSITY PRESS
1939

CAMBRIDGE UNIVERSITY PRESS
Cambridge, New York, Melbourne, Madrid, Cape Town, Singapore,
São Paulo, Delhi, Dubai, Tokyo, Mexico City

Cambridge University Press
The Edinburgh Building, Cambridge CB2 8RU, UK

Published in the United States of America by Cambridge University Press, New York

www.cambridge.org
Information on this title: www.cambridge.org/9780521166331

First published 1939
First paperback edition 2010

A catalogue record for this publication is available from the British Library

ISBN 978-0-521-16633-1 Paperback

To the Memory of

PETER WARLOCK
(PHILIP HESELTINE)
1894–1930

*whose Songs and Music
are in the true
English Tradition*

Whatever prosperity may return to our country places, it will not be on the old terms. The 'few reforms', whether in the direction of import duties, or small holdings, or 'technical education' in ploughing or fruit-pruning or forestry or sheep-shearing, can never in themselves be a substitute for the lost peasant traditions, because they are not the same kind of thing. For those traditions were no institutions set up and cherished by outside authority. Associated though they were with industrial and material well-being, they meant much more than that to country folk; they lived in the popular tastes and habits, and they passed on spontaneously from generation to generation, as a sort of rural civilization. And you cannot treat that sort of thing by Act of Parliament, or by juggling with tariffs, or by school lessons.

GEORGE BOURNE, *Change in the Village* (1912)

CONTENTS

  * The three parts correspond to the division of topics in the List
on pages 153–4.

PART TWO

PART THREE

ILLUSTRATIONS

INTRODUCTION

In every farmyard, outhouse and contingent building throughout
the country are to be seen—piled-up relics of past generations of
farmers—the remains of old ploughs, waggons and implements
crumbling away behind the new steam-thresher and brightly-painted
iron rakes and harrows.*

WHEN, to-day, we happen to turn our thoughts to
the life and work of the English countryside, we
cannot but reflect that it is not only the ancient implements
of village labour that are fast crumbling away behind the
new, but that the whole village mode of living and experience is changing or vanishing. Apart from some knowledge of, and sympathy with that ancient mode, the essential
nature of English culture hitherto cannot be properly understood or explained; but it has been disintegrating so fast
during the last two or three generations that the modern
schoolboy, when he comes to choosing his career, may not
even hear of its existence.

For the twentieth century the terms Culture and Agriculture connote entirely different, unrelated worlds. It is
the aim of this book to suggest that this antithesis is false.
It is no accident that the words themselves suggest a
relation: the one is an integral part of the other, agriculture
a particular branch of a general discipline (or civilization).
True culture cannot exist without the contribution of the
many particular physical disciplines (as we may call the old
country crafts)—agriculture is the central one—which are
its roots and guarantee its fertility. The selections in this
book give some account of rural industries as they used to

* Hennell, *Change in the Farm*.

flourish before 'big business' and mechanization developed from a position in which they merely threatened their existence (we can see this threat plainly in several of the passages), to one in which they obtained a stranglehold upon them. The authors chosen describe other country arts and crafts besides those actually practised on farms, and some of them dwell on more general aspects of country life, but in all their writings a comparatively sound and healthy condition of agriculture is implied; it may be doubted whether that condition has been able in any real sense to survive the pressure of modern 'progress'. This is not to say that working conditions and wages have not improved beyond recognition for many individual labourers and perhaps some few craftsmen, especially since the Great War, nor do all authors qualified to speak take a pessimistic view of the future—Mr Adrian Bell seems quite hopeful in his *By-road*, and the Government supports an active Rural Industries Bureau. It seems clear, however, that the old garment, carefully as we may patch it up, must soon become unrecognizable for what it was, and that whatever takes its place will be radically a different thing.

What was it that the traditional conditions of rural life, with all their glaring imperfections, guaranteed to English civilization? We may describe it as a sense of *community*, a sense which was no less real and potent because it was unconscious, taken for granted by those who possessed it. The countryman's horizon was narrow; he was often described as a 'boor', in many instances rightly so, as we can see in several essays by Richard Jefferies. But Jefferies' admiration for the life and work of the countryside must have been based upon some positive and inherent values. In his Preface to *Round About a Great Estate* he says:

My sympathies and hopes are with the light of the future, only I should like it to come from nature. In this book some notes have been made of the former state of things before it passes away entirely. But I would not have it therefore thought that I wish it to continue or return.... The clock should be read by the sunshine, not the sun timed by the clock. The latter is indeed impossible, for though all the clocks in the world should declare the hour of dawn to be midnight, the sun will presently rise just the same.

Elementary schooling was, of course, eventually secured by Act of Parliament. Well-meaning educationists attempted to introduce further cultural enlightenment among adult villagers. Jefferies saw the beginnings of this movement: his comment was, 'For the enjoyment of art it is first of all necessary to have a full belly.' In fact, economic conditions had not fundamentally changed since the eighteenth century, the period that inspired Goldsmith's *The Deserted Village*:

> Ill fares the land, to hast'ning ills a prey,
> Where wealth accumulates, and men decay.

They remained unchanged. A writer in 1913 begins a book on *Problems of Village Life* with a chapter which is still a prose counterpart of Goldsmith's poem.* The War forced some few changes, but even to-day a satisfactory settlement for agriculture is still unfound. New forces, largely bound up with economic changes, have come with startling rapidity to bear on rural life and labour; pre-War answers to the problems, however intelligent and farseeing those

* By E. N. Bennett, Home University Library, now unfortunately out of print. It is remarkable how much of what the author wrote in 1913 sounds 'modern' now. Compare *The Changing Village*, by F. G. Thomas (1939).

who suggested them may have been, would need such drastic revision that their application seems as remote as ever. We are still far behind a solution of our difficulties, as the nineteenth century was behind with its comparatively simpler ones.

This is not the place to enter into a detailed discussion of the relations between culture and environment, and the reasons for the evident decay in culture due to the nature of the environment in twentieth-century England (and elsewhere). It has been done by Dr F. R. Leavis and Mr Denys Thompson in a book which should be read by all who are interested in the implications of this anthology.* Here we are concerned with this culture only up to the time when it *began* to show signs of disintegration. For village workers and craftsmen did possess 'art', though of a kind different from that referred to by Richard Jefferies. It is this that George Sturt, or 'Bourne', is discussing when he says:

A good wheelwright knew by art but not by reasoning the proportion to keep between spokes and felloes; and so too a good smith knew how tight a two-and-a-half inch tyre should be made for a five-foot wheel and how tight for a four-foot, and so on. He felt it, in his bones. It was a perception with him. But there was no science in it; no reasoning. Every detail stood by itself, and had to be learnt either by trial and error or by tradition....

In watching Cook put a wheel together I was watching practically the skill of England, the experience of ages.

* *Culture and Environment: The Training of Critical Awareness,* Chatto and Windus, 3s. 6d. See particularly the chapters on 'Tradition', 'The Organic Community' and 'The Loss of the Organic Community'. The volume contains an excellent bibliography (to 1933).

All the crafts described in this book depended for their success and virtue on being each the result of the 'picked experience of ages', and as such they cannot be replaced. No products of a machine age, no 'efficiency', can make up for their disappearance:

Tradition may have been superseded in industry and economic life, but it cannot be superseded in everything, unless our culture is to die. Such a craft as the wheel-wright's, embodying the experience of centuries, was a part of the national culture, along with the time-honoured ways of living and the inherited wisdom of the folk. At the centre of our culture is language, and while we have our language, tradition is, in some essential sense, still alive.*

Whether we can succeed in keeping our language in living contact with 'tradition' in this sense is a major question with the few responsible critics writing to-day; that the authors represented in this book succeeded in doing so, though without conscious effort, is their chief claim to our attention.

Writers on style emphasize the fact that the more intimate the knowledge of the subject, the better the writing is likely to be. Poor writing comes from lack of observation and interest, or ignorance of the subject. If any proof of this is needed, it will be found in the extracts in this book. There is no 'fine writing', no attempt to create effects for their own sake. The writers represented here have plenty to say about their own daily work and experiences; they have written naturally and clearly about their own lives, and the result is good sound English prose—simple, unaffected and well fitted to its matter.

The interest of these writings comes from the interesting lives and work of the authors—their occupations demanded

* *Culture and Environment*, p. 80.

more than a limited 'technical' knowledge, and therefore their books are not mere manuals on wheel-making, farming, or carpentry. After all, do we ever think of a farmer as a 'technical' worker? His life is too varied for that. *The Wheelwright's Shop*, for instance, does not demand any specialized knowledge on the part of the reader; it makes itself clear as it goes along. Nor, though it makes us realize the importance and value of rural industry, does it make us want to go out and make wheels after we have read it; in other words, it is not propaganda. But who would read a motor-car manual for pleasure, except those who make a special hobby of that sort of thing? and what chance would the layman have of understanding it? The difference between *The Wheelwright's Shop* and the motor manual is the difference between literature and technical writing; perhaps it is the difference between two civilizations.

One last word: we shall have failed in our purpose if a reading of this book does not lead to a reading of the complete works of the men from whom selections have been taken; a list of their most important books, and suggestions for supplementary reading will be found on page 154.

ACKNOWLEDGMENTS

Our special thanks are due to the staff of the Cambridge University Press for suggestions and encouragement without which the book would have been impossible in its present form.

Mr Hutchinson has received valuable bibliographical assistance from his father, Mr G. R. Hutchinson, Mr

Charles H. Barber (President of the Association of Book-sellers of Great Britain and Ireland), and Mr H. Peers (at one of the pleasantest bookshops in Manchester); Mr Chapman has been saved many laborious hours by the help of Mrs de Voil in typing certain passages.

Acknowledgment of permission to make use of material from copyright works is made to the following publishers: Messrs Cobden-Sanderson (Adrian Bell, *By-Road*), Messrs Gerald Duckworth (George Bourne, *Memoirs of a Surrey Labourer* and *Lucy Bettesworth*), Messrs Faber and Faber (A. G. Street, *Farmer's Glory*), Messrs Victor Gollancz (H. E. Bates, *Down the River*), Messrs Methuen (Richard Jefferies, *Hodge and his Masters*), Messrs John Murray (Richard Jefferies, *Round About a Great Estate*), and the Cambridge University Press (T. Hennell, *Change in the Farm*; G. Sturt, *The Wheelwright's Shop*; W. Rose, *The Village Carpenter*).

C.G.H.

AUGUST 1939   F.C.

PART ONE

I

A FARMER OF THE OLDEN TIMES

By RICHARD JEFFERIES

AFTER hearing Hilary talk so much of old Jonathan I thought I should like to see the place where he had lived, and later in the season walked up on the hills for that purpose. The stunted fir-trees on the Down gave so little shadow that I was glad to find a hawthorn under whose branches I could rest on the sward. The prevalent winds of winter sweeping without check along the open slope had bent the hawthorn before them, and the heat of the sultry summer day appeared the greater on that exposed height. On either hand hills succeeded to hills, and behind I knew they extended farther than the eye could reach. Immediately beneath in front there was a plain, at its extreme boundary a wood, and beyond that the horizon was lost in the summer haze. Wheat, barley, and oats—barley and wheat and beans, completely occupied the plain. It was one vast expanse of cereals, without a sign of human life; for the reaper had not yet commenced, and the bailiffs' cottages were hidden among the ricks. There was an utter silence at noonday; nothing but yellowing wheat beneath, the ramparts of the hills around, and the sun above.

But, though out of sight, there was a farmhouse behind a small copse and clump of elms full of rooks' nests, a short way from the foot of the Down. This was 'The Idovers', once the residence of old Jonathan; it was the last farm before reaching the hill district proper, and from the slope here all the fields of which it consisted were visible. The house was small, for in those days farmers did not look to live in villas, and till within the last few years even the parlour floor was of stone flags. Rushes used to be strewn in the halls of palaces in ancient times, and seventy years ago old Jonathan grew his own carpets.

The softest and best of the bean straw grown on the farm was selected and scattered on the floor of the sitting-rooms as warm and dry to the feet, and that was all the carpet in the house. Just before sheep-shearing time, too, Jonathan used to have the nettles cut that flourished round the back of the sheds, and strewn on the floor of the barn. The nettles shrivelled up dry, and the wool did not stick to them, but could be gathered easily.

With his own hands he would carry out a quart of beans to the pigs—just a quart at a time and no more, that they might eat every one and that none might be wasted. So, too, he would carry them a few acorns in his coat pocket, and watch the relish with which the swine devoured their favourite food. He saved every bit of crooked wood that was found about the place; for at that date iron was expensive, and wood that had grown crooked and was therefore strong as well as curved was useful for a hundred purposes. Fastened to a wall, for instance, it did for a hook upon which to hang things. If an apple tree died in the orchard it was cut out to form part of a plough and saved till wanted.

Jonathan's hard head withstood even the whirl of the days when corn was at famine prices. But these careful economies, this continual saving, put more money in his purse than all that sudden flush of prosperity. Every groat thus saved was as a nail driven into an oak, fixed and stable, becoming firmer as time went on. How strangely different the farmers of to-day, with a score of machines and appliances, with expensive feeding stuffs, with well-furnished villas! Each one of Jonathan's beans in his quart mug, each one of the acorns in his pocket became a guinea.

Jonathan's hat was made to measure on his own special block by the hatter in Overboro' town, and it was so hard and stout that he could sit upon it without injury. His top-boots always hung near the fire-place, that they might not get mouldy; and he rode into market upon his 'short-tail horse', as he called his crop-tail nag. A farmer was nothing thought of unless he wore top-boots, which seemed a distinguishing mark, as it were, of the equestrian order of agriculture.

But his shoes were made straight; not as now, one to each foot—a right and left—but each exactly alike; and he changed his shoes every morning, wearing one on one foot one day and on the other the next, that they might not get worn to either foot in particular. Shoes lasted a great length of time in those days, the leather being all tanned with oak bark only, and thoroughly seasoned before it was cut up. There is even a story of a farmer who wore his best shoes every Sunday for seven years in Sundays—fifty years—and when he died had them buried with him, still far from worn out.

A traveller once returned from America—in those days a very far-off land—and was recounting the wonders he had seen, and among them how the folk there used sleighs, not only for driving in but for the removal of heavy goods. But Jonathan did not think it strange, since when he was young wheeled vehicles were not so common. He had himself seen loads of hay drawn home on 'sleds' from English meadows, and could tell where a 'sled' had last been used. There were aged men living about the hamlet in his day—if that could be called a hamlet in which there were barely a score of people, all told—who could recollect when the first waggon came to 'The Idovers'. At all events, they pointed out a large field, called the Conigers, where it was taken to turn it round; for it was constructed in so primitive a style that the forewheels would not pass under the body, and thus required a whole field to turn in.

At that date folk had no banking accounts, but kept their coin in a strong chest under the bed, sometimes hiding it in strange places. Jonathan was once visiting a friend, and after they had hobnobbed a while the old fellow took him, with many precautions that they should not be observed, into the pigsty and showed him fifty guineas hid in the thatch. That was by no means all his property, but the old fellow said, with a wink, that he liked to have a little hoard of his own that his wife knew nothing about.

Some land being put up for sale, after biddings by the well-to-do residents, an old dealer in a very small way, as was supposed, bid above them all. The company looked upon him with contempt, and his offer was regarded as mere folly; but he produced a nail-bag from under his coat and counted out the money. A nail-bag is made of the coarsest of all kinds of sacking. In this manner the former generation, eschewing outward show, collected their money coin by coin, till at last they became substantial men and owners of real estate. So few were the conveniences of life that men had often to leave the road and cross several fields out of their way to light their pipes at a burning couch-heap or lime-kiln.

They prided themselves then in that hill district that they had neither a cow nor a poor married man in the parish. There was no cow, because it was entirely a corn-growing place. The whole resident population was not much over a score, and of the labourers they boasted not one was married. For in those old times each parish kept its own poor, and consequently disliked an increase of the population. The farmers met in vestry from time to time to arrange for the support of the surplus labour; the appearance of a fresh family would have meant a fresh tax upon them. They regarded additional human beings as an incumbrance.

The millers sent their flour round the country then on packhorses; waggons and carts were not so common as now, while the ways, when you once quitted the main road, were scarcely passable. Even the main roads were often in such a state that foot-passengers could not get along, but left the road and followed a footpath just inside the hedge. Such footpaths ran beside the roads for miles; here and there in country places a short section of such tracks may still be found. 'Pack-roads', too, may be occasionally met with, retaining their designation to this day. It was the time of the great wars with the First Napoleon; and the poor people, as the wheat went up to famine prices, were often in a strait for bread. When the miller's packhorse appeared the cottagers crowded round and demanded the price: if it had risen a penny, the infuriated mob of women would sometimes pull the miller's boy off the horse and duck him in the village pond.

The memory of those old times is still vivid in farmhouses, and at Hilary's I have myself handled old Jonathan's walking-staff, which he and his father before him used in traversing on foot those perilous roads. It was about five feet long, perhaps more, an inch and a half in diameter, and shod with an iron ferrule and stout spike. With this he could prod the sloughs and ascertain their depth, or use it as a leaping-pole; and if threatened by sturdy rogues whirl it about their heads as a quarter-staff.

Wars and famines were then terrible realities—men's minds were full of them, and superstition flourished. The foggers and shepherds saw signs in the sky and read the stars. Down at Lucketts' Place one winter's night, when folk almost fancied they could hear the roar of Napoleon's cannon, the old fogger came rushing in with the news that the armies could be seen fighting in the heavens. It was an aurora, the streamers shooting up towards the zenith, and great red spots among the stars, the ghastly stains of the wounded. The old fogger declared that as he went out with his lantern to attend to the cows calving he could see the blood dripping on the back of his hand as it fell down from the battling hosts above.

To us the ignorance even of such comparatively recent times is almost incredible. As Hilary was telling me of such things as we sat in his house one evening, there grew upon our ears a peculiar sound, a humming deep bass, somewhat resembling the low notes of a piano with a pressure on the pedal. It increased and became louder, coming from the road which passed the house; it was caused by a very large flock of sheep driven slowly. The individual 'baa' of each lamb was so mixed, as it were, with the bleat of its fellow that the swelling sound took a strange, mysterious tone; a voice that seemed to speak of trouble, and perplexity, and anxiety for rest. Hilary, as a farmer, must of course go out to see whose they were, and I went with him; but before he reached the garden gate he turned back, remarking, 'It's Johnson's flock; I know the tang of his tankards.' The flat-shaped bells hung on a sheep's neck are called tankards; and Hilary could distinguish one flock from another by the varying notes of their bells.

Reclining on the sweet short sward under the hawthorn on the Down I looked over the Idover plain, and thought of the olden times. As I gazed I presently observed, far away beside some ricks, the short black funnel of an engine, and made it out to be a steam plough waiting till the corn should be garnered to tear up the stubble. How much meaning there lay in the presence of that black funnel! There were the same broad open fields, the same beautiful crops of golden wheat, the same green hills, and the same sun ripening the grain. But how strangely changed all human affairs since old Jonathan, in his straight-made shoes, with his pike-staff, and the acorns in his pocket, trudged along the footpaths!

RICHARD JEFFERIES, *Round About a Great Estate* (1880)

II

THE 'GENTLEMAN' FARMER
A HUNDRED YEARS AGO

By WILLIAM COBBETT

REIGATE
Thursday Evening, 20 *October* 1825

HAVING done my business at Hartswood to-day about eleven o'clock, I went to a sale at a farm, which the farmer is quitting. Here I had a view of what has long been going on all over the country. The farm, which belongs to *Christ's Hospital,* has been held by a man of the name of Charington, in whose family the lease has been, I hear, a great number of years. The house is hidden by trees. It stands in the Weald of Surrey, close by the *River Mole,* which is here a mere rivulet, though just below this house the rivulet supplies the very prettiest flour-mill I ever saw in my life.

Everything about this farmhouse was formerly the scene of *plain manners* and *plentiful living.* Oak clothes-chests, oak bedsteads, oak chests of drawers, and oak tables to eat on, long, strong, and well supplied with joint stools. Some of the things were many hundreds of years old. But all appeared to be in a state of decay and nearly of *disuse.* There appeared to have been hardly any *family* in that house, where formerly there were, in all probability, from ten to fifteen men, boys, and maids: and, which was the worst of all, there was a *parlour.* Aye, and a *carpet* and *bell-pull* too! One end of the front of this once plain and substantial house had been moulded into a '*parlour*'; and there was the mahogany table, and the fine chairs, and the fine glass, and all as barefaced upstart as any stock-jobber in the kingdom can boast of. And there were the decanters, the glasses, the 'dinner-set' of crockery-ware, and all just in the true stock-jobber style. And I dare say it has been *'Squire* Charington and the *Miss* Charington's; and not plain Master Charington, and his son Hodge, and his daughter Betty Charington, all of whom this accursed system has, in all likelihood, transmuted into a species of mock gentlefolks, while it has ground the labourers down into real slaves. Why do not farmers now *feed* and *lodge* their workpeople, as they did formerly? Because they cannot keep them *upon so little* as they give them in wages. This is the real cause of the change. There needs no more to prove that the lot of the working classes has become worse than it formerly was. This fact alone is quite sufficient to settle this point. All the world knows that a number of people, boarded in the same house, and at the same table, can, with as good food, be boarded much cheaper than those persons divided into twos, threes, or fours, can be boarded. This is a well-known truth: therefore, if the farmer now shuts his pantry against his labourers, and pays them wholly in money, is it not clear that he does it because he thereby gives them a living *cheaper* to him; that is to say, a *worse* living than formerly? Mind, he has *a house* for them; a kitchen for them to sit in, bedrooms for them to sleep in, tables and stools, and benches, of everlasting duration. All these he has: all these *cost him nothing*; and yet so much does he gain by pinching them in wages that he lets all these things remain as of no use rather than feed labourers in the house. Judge, then, of the *change* that has taken place in the condition of these labourers! And be astonished, if you can, at the *pauperism* and the *crimes* that now disgrace this once happy and moral England.

The land produces, on an average, what it always produced, but there is a new distribution of the produce. This 'Squire Charington's father used, I dare say, to sit at the head of the oak table along with his men, say grace to them, and cut up the meat and the pudding. He might take a cup of *strong beer* to himself, when they had none; but that was pretty nearly all the difference in their manner of living. So that *all* lived well. But the 'squire had many *wine-decanters* and *wine-glasses* and '*a dinner set*', and a '*breakfast set*', and '*dessert knives*'; and these evidently imply carryings on and a consumption that must of necessity have greatly robbed the long oak table if it had remained fully tenanted. That long table could not share in the work of the decanters and the dinner set. Therefore, it became almost untenanted; the labourers retreated to hovels, called cottages; and instead of board and lodging, they got money; so little of it as to enable the employer to drink wine; but, then, that he might not reduce them to *quite starvation*, they were enabled to come to him, in the *king's name*, and demand food *as paupers*. And now, mind, that which a man receives in the *king's name*, he knows well he has *by force*; and it is not in nature that he should *thank* anybody for it, and least of all the party *from whom it is forced*. Then, if this sort of force be insufficient to obtain him enough to eat and to keep him warm, is it surprising if he think it no great offence against God (who created no man to starve) to use another sort of force more within his own control? Is it, in short, surprising, if he resort to *theft* and *robbery*?

This is not only the *natural* progress, but it *has been* the progress in England. The blame is not justly imputed to

'Squire Charington and his like: the blame belongs to the infernal stock-jobbing system. There was no reason to expect that farmers would not endeavour to keep pace, in point of show and luxury, with fund-holders, and with all the tribes that *war* and *taxes* created. Farmers were not the authors of the mischief; and *now* they are compelled to shut the labourers out of their houses, and to pinch them in their wages, in order to be able to pay their own taxes; and, besides this, the manners and the principles of the working class are so changed that a sort of self-preservation bids the farmer (especially in some counties) to keep them from beneath his roof.

I could not quit the farmhouse without reflecting on the thousands of scores of bacon and thousands of bushels of bread that had been eaten from the long oak table which, I said to myself, is now perhaps going at last to the bottom of a bridge that some stock-jobber will stick up over an artificial river in his cockney garden. '*By —— it shan't,'* said I, almost in a real passion: and so I requested a friend to buy it for me; and if he do so, I will take it to Kensington, or to Fleet Street, and keep it for the good it has done in the world.

When the old farmhouses are down (and down they must come in time) what a miserable thing the country will be! Those that are now erected are mere painted shells, with a mistress within, who is stuck up in a place she calls a *parlour*, with, if she have children, the 'young ladies and gentlemen' about her: some showy chairs and a sofa (a *sofa* by all means): half a dozen prints in gilt frames hanging up: some swinging bookshelves with novels and tracts upon them: a dinner brought in by a girl that is perhaps better 'educated' than she: two or three nick-nacks to eat instead of a piece of bacon and a pudding: the house too neat for a dirty-shoed carter to be allowed to come into; and everything proclaiming to every sensible beholder that there is here a constant anxiety to make a *show* not warranted by the reality. The children (which is the worst part of it) are all too clever to *work*: they are all to be *gentlefolks*. Go to plough! Good God! What, 'young gentlemen' go to plough! They become *clerks*, or some skimmydish thing or other. They flee from the dirty *work* as cunning horses do from the bridle. What misery is all this! What a mass of materials for producing that general and *dreadful convulsion* that must, first or last, come and blow this funding and jobbing and enslaving and starving system to atoms!

WILLIAM COBBETT, *Rural Rides* (1830)

III

FLEECEBOROUGH

By RICHARD JEFFERIES

FARMERS have long since discovered that it is best to rent under a very large owner, whether personal, or impersonal as a college or corporation. A very large owner like this can be, and is, more liberal. He puts up sheds, and he drains, and improves, and builds good cottages for the labourers. Provided, of course, that no serious malpractice comes to light, he, as represented by his steward, never interferes, and the tenant is personally free. No one watches his goings out and his comings in; he has no sense of an eye for ever looking over the park wall. There is a total absence of the grasping spirit sometimes shown. The farmer does not feel that he will be worried to his last shilling. In case of unfavourable seasons the landlord makes no difficulty in returning a portion of the rent; he anticipates such an application. Such immense possessions can support losses which would press most heavily upon comparatively small properties. At one side of the estate the soil perchance is light and porous, and is all the better for rain; on the other, half across the county, or quite, the soil is deep and heavy and naturally well watered and flourishes in dry summers. So that there is generally some one prospering if another suffers, and thus a balance is maintained.

A reserve of wealth has, too, slowly accumulated in the family coffers, which, in exceptional years, tides the owner over with little or no appreciable inconvenience. With an income like this, special allowances, even generous allowances, can be, and are made, and so the tenants cease to feel that their landlord is living out of their labour. The agreements are just; there is no rapacity. Very likely the original lease or arrangement has expired half a century since; but no one troubles to renew it. It is well understood that no change will be effected. The tenure is as steady as if the tenant had an Act of Parliament at his back.

When men have once settled, they and their descendants remain, generation after generation. By degrees their sons and sons' descendants settle too, and the same name occurs perhaps in a dozen adjacent places. It is this fixed unchangeable character of the district which has enabled the mass of the tenants not indeed to become wealthy, but to acquire a solid, substantial standing. In farming affairs money can be got together only in the slow passage of years; experience has proved that beyond a doubt. These people have been stationary for a length of time, and the moss of the proverb has grown around them. They walk sturdily, and look all men in the face; their fathers put money in the purse. Times are hard here as everywhere, but if they cannot, for the present season, put more in that purse, its contents are not, at all events, much diminished, and enable them to maintain the same straightforward manliness and independence. By-and-by, they know there will come the chink of the coin again.

When the tenant is stationary, the labourer is also. He stays in the same cottage on the same farm all his life, his descendants remain and work for the same tenant family. He can trace his descent in the locality for a hundred years. From time immemorial both Hodge and his immediate employers have looked towards Fleeceborough as their capital. Hodge goes into the market in charge of his master's sheep, his wife trudges in for household necessaries. All the hamlet goes in to the annual fairs. Every cottager in the hamlet knows somebody in the town; the girls go there to service, the boys to get employment. The little village shops obtain their goods from thence. All the produce—wheat, barley, oats, hay, cattle, and sheep, is sent into the capital to the various markets held there. The very ideas held in the villages by the inhabitants come from Fleeceborough; the local papers published there are sold all round, and supply them with news, arguments, and the politics of the little kingdom. The farmers look to Fleeceborough just as much or more. It is a religious duty to be seen there on market days. Not a man misses being there; if he is not visible, his circle note it, and guess at various explanations.

Each man has his own particular hostelry, where his father, and his grandfather, put up before him, and where he is expected to dine in the same old room, with the pictures of famous rams, that have fetched fabulous prices, framed against the walls, and rams' horns of exceptional size and peculiar curve fixed up above the mantelpiece. Men come in in groups of two or three, as dinner time approaches, and chat about sheep and wool, and wool and sheep; but no one finally settles himself at the table till the chairman arrives. He is a stout, substantial farmer, who has dined there every market day for the last thirty or forty years.

Everybody has his own particular seat, which he is certain to find kept for him. The dinner itself is simple enough, the waiters perhaps still more simple, but the quality of the viands is beyond praise. The mutton is juicy and delicious, as it should be where the sheep is the idol of all men's thoughts; the beef is short and tender of grain; the vegetables, nothing can equal them, and they are here, asparagus and all, in profusion. The landlord grows his own vegetables—every householder in Fleeceborough has an ample garden—and produces the fruit from his own orchards for the tarts. Ever and anon a waiter walks round with a can of ale and fills the glasses, whether asked or not. Beef and mutton, vegetables and fruit tarts, and ale are simple and plain fare, but when they are served in the best form, how will you surpass them? The real English cheese, the fresh salads, the exquisite butter—everything on the table is genuine, juicy, succulent, and rich. Could such a dinner be found in London, how the folk would crowd thither! Finally, comes the waiter with his two clean plates, the upper one to receive the money, the lower to retain what is his. If you are a stranger, and remember what you have been charged elsewhere in smoky cities for tough beef, stringy mutton, waxy potatoes, and the very bread black with smuts, you select half a sovereign and drop it on the upper plate. In the twinkling of an eye eight shillings are returned to you; the charge is a florin only.

They live well in Fleeceborough, as every fresh experience of the place will prove; they have plentiful food, and of the best quality; poultry abounds, for every resident having a great garden (many, too, have paddocks) keeps fowls; fresh eggs are common; as for vegetables and fruit, the abundance is not to be described. And their ale! To the first sight it is not tempting. It is thick, dark, a deep wine colour; a slight aroma arises from it like that which dwells in bonded warehouses. The first taste is not pleasing; but it induces a second, and a third. By-and-by the flavour grows upon the palate; and now beware, for if a small quantity be thrown upon the fire it will blaze up with a blue flame like pure alcohol. That dark, vinous-looking ale is full of the strength of malt and hops; it is the brandy of the barley. The unwary find their heads curiously queer before they have partaken, as it seems to them, of a couple of glasses. The very spirit and character of Fleeceborough is embodied in the ale; rich, strong, genuine. No one knows what English ale is till he has tried this.

After the market dinner the guests sit still—they do not hurry away to counter and desk; they rest a while, and dwell as it were, on the flavour of their food. There is a hum of pleasant talk, for each man is a right boon companion. The burden of that talk has been the same for generations— sheep and wool, wool and sheep. Occasionally mysterious allusions are made to 'he', what 'he' will do with a certain farm, whether 'he' will support such and such a movement, or subscribe to some particular fund, what view will 'he' take of the local question of the day? Perhaps some one has had special information of the step 'he' is likely to take; then that favoured man is an object of the deepest interest, and is cross-questioned all round the table till his small item of authentic intelligence has been thoroughly assimilated. 'He' is the resident within those vast and endless walls, with the metal gates and the gilded coronet above—the prince of this kingdom and its capital city. To see rightly the subjects loyally hastening thither, let any- one ascend the church tower on market day.

It is remarkably high, and from thence the various roads converging on the town are visible. The province lies stretched out beneath. There is the gleam of water—the little river, with its ancient mills—that flows beside the town; there are the meadows, with their pleasant footpaths. Yonder the ploughed fields and woods, and yet more distant the open hills. Along every road, and there are many, the folk are hastening to their capital city, in gigs, on horseback, in dog-traps and four-wheels, or sturdily trudging afoot. The breeze comes sweet and exhilarating from the hills and over the broad acres and green woods; it strikes the chest as you lean against the parapet, and the jackdaws suspend themselves in mid-air with outstretched wings upheld by its force. For how many years, how many centuries, has this little town and this district around it been distinct and separate? In the days before the arrival of the Roman legions it was the country of a distinct tribe, or nation, of the original Britons. But if we speak of history we shall never have done, for the town and its antique abbey (of which this tower is a mere remnant) have mingled more or less in every change that has occurred, down from the earthwork camp yonder on the hills to to-day—down to the last puff of the locomotive there below, as its driver shuts off steam and runs in with passengers and dealers for the market, with the papers, and the latest novel from London.

Something of the old local patriotism survives, and is vigorous in the town here. Men marry in the place, find their children employment in the place, and will not move, if they can help it. Their families—well-to-do and humble alike—have been there for so many, many years. The very carter, or the little tailor working in his shop-window, will tell you (and prove to you by records) that his ancestor stood to the barricade with pike or matchlock when the army of King or Parliament, as the case may be, besieged the sturdy town two hundred years ago. He has a longer pedigree than many a titled dweller in Belgravia. All these people believe in Fleeceborough. When fate forces them to quit—when the young man seeks his fortune in New Zealand or America—he writes home the fullest information, and his letters published in the local print read curiously to an outsider, so full are they of local inquiries, and answers to friends who wished to know this or that. In the end he comes back—should he succeed in getting the gold which tempted him away—to pass his latter days in gossiping round with the dear old folk, and to marry amongst them. Yet, with all their deep local patriotism, they are not bigoted or narrow-minded; there is too much literature abroad for that, and they have the cosiest reading-room wherein to learn all that passes in the world. They have a town council held now and then in an ancient wainscoted hall, with painted panels and coats of arms, carved oaken seats black with age, and narrow windows from which men once looked down into the street, wearing trunk hose and rapier.

But they have at least two other councils that meet much more often, and that meet by night. When his books are balanced, when his shop is shut, after he has strolled round his garden, and taken his supper, the tradesman or shopkeeper walks down to his inn, and there finds his circle assembled. They are all there, the rich and the moderately well-to-do, the struggling, and the poor. Each delivers his opinion over the social glass, or between the deliberate puffs of his cigar or pipe. The drinking is extremely moderate, the smoking not quite so temperate; but neither the glass nor the cigar are the real attractions. It is the common hall— the informal place of meeting.

It is here that the real government of the town is planned

—the more formal resolutions voted in the ancient council-room are the outcome of the open talk, and the quiet whisper here. No matter what subject is to the front, the question is always heard—What will 'he' do? What will 'he' say to it? The Volunteers compete for prizes which 'he' offers. The cottage hospital; the flower show; the cattle show, or agricultural exhibition; the new market buildings arose through his subscriptions and influence; the artesian well, sunk that the town might have the best of water, was bored at his expense; and so on through the whole list of town affairs. When 'he' takes the lead all the lesser gentry—many of whom, perhaps, live in his manor houses—follow suit, and with such powerful support to back it a movement is sure to succeed, yet 'he' is rarely seen; his hand rarely felt; everything is done, but without obtrusiveness. At these nightly councils at the chief hostelries the farmers of the district are almost as numerous as the townsmen. They ride in to hear the news and exchange their own small coin of gossip. They want to know what 'he' is going to do, and little by little of course it leaks out.

But the town is not all so loyal. There is a section which is all the more vehemently rebellious because of the spectacle of its staid and comfortable neighbours. This section is very small, but makes a considerable noise. It holds meetings and denounces the 'despot' in fiery language. It protests against a free and open park; it abhors artesian wells; it detests the throwing open of nut woods that all may go forth a-nutting; it waxes righteously indignant at every gift, be it prizes for the flower show or a new market site. It scorns those mean-spirited citizens that cheer these kindly deeds. It asks why? Why should we

wait till the park gates are open? Why stay till the nut
woods are declared ready? Why be thankful for pure
water? Why not take our own? This one man has no right
to these parks and woods and pleasure grounds and vast
walls; these square miles of ploughed fields, meadows and
hills. By right they should all be split up into little plots
to grow our potatoes. Away with gilded coronet and
watchman, batter down these walls, burn the ancient deeds
and archives, put pick and lever to the tall church tower;
let us have the rights of man! These violent ebullitions
make not the least difference. All the insults they can
devise, all the petty obstructions they can set up, the mud
they can fling, does not alter the calm course of the 'despot'
one jot. The artesian well is bored, and they can drink pure
water or not, as pleases them. The prizes are offered, and
they can compete or stand aloof. Fleeceborough smiles
when it meets at night in its council-rooms, with its glass
and pipe; Fleeceborough knows that the traditional policy
of the Hall will continue, and that policy is acceptable to it.

What manner of man is this 'despot' and prince behind
his vast walls? Verily his physique matters nothing;
whether he be old or of middle age, tall or short, infirm or
strong. The policy of the house keeps the actual head and
owner rather in the background. His presence is never
obtruded; he is rarely seen; you may stay in his capital for
months and never catch a glimpse of him. He will not
appear at meetings, that every man may be free, not
hesitate to say his say, and abuse what he lists to abuse.
The policy is simply perfect freedom with support and
substantial assistance to any and to every movement set
on foot by the respectable men of Fleeceborough, or by the
tenant-farmers round about. This has been going on for

generations; so that the *personnel* of the actual owner concerns little. His predecessors did it, he does it, and the next to come will do it. It is the tradition of the house. Nothing is left undone that a truly princely spirit could do to improve, to beautify, or to preserve.

The antiquities of the old, old town are kept for it, and not permitted to decay; the ancient tessellated pavements of Roman villas carefully protected from the weather; the remnants of the enclosing walls which the legions built for their defence saved from destruction; the coins of the emperors and of our own early kings collected; the spurs, swords, spearheads, all the fragments of past ages arranged for inspection and study by every one who desires to ponder over them. Chipped flints and arrowheads, the bones of animals long extinct, and the strange evidences of yet more ancient creatures that swam in the seas of the prehistoric world, these too are preserved at his cost and expense. Archaeologists, geologists, and other men of science come from afar to see these things and to carry away their lessons. The memories of the place are cherished. There was a famous poet who sang in the woods about the park; his hermitage remains, and nothing is lost that was his. Art treasures there are, too, heirlooms to be seen behind those vast walls by any who will be at the trouble of asking.

Such is the policy of Hodge's own prince, whose silent influence is felt in every household for miles about, and felt, as all must admit, however prejudiced against the system, in this case for good. His influence reaches far beyond the bounds even of that immense property. The example communicates itself to others, and half the county responds to that pleasant impulse. It is a responsible position to hold; something, perhaps, a little like that of the Medici at Florence in the olden times. But here there is no gonfalon, no golden chain of office, no velvet doublet, cloak, and rapier, no guards with arquebus or polished crossbow. An entire absence of state and ceremony marks this almost unseen but powerful sway. The cycle of the seasons brings round times of trial here as over the entire world, but the conditions under which the trial is sustained could scarcely in our day, and under our complicated social and political system, be much more favourable.

RICHARD JEFFERIES, *Hodge and his Masters* (1880)

IV

MODERN TIMES

By A. G. STREET

GENERALLY speaking, the older labourers longed for the times of long ago in spite of their increased prosperity. 'But times are better for the men now,' I said to a rugged old-age pensioner one day, when we were discussing rural affairs. 'Look at the wages they get.'

''Tidn what they gets. What do 'em earn? Why, when I wor a young man I wor worth dree ov 'em. Do make I fair voam at mouth to zee zum ov 'em fiddlin' about at their work.'

I met this same critic of modern times only last week, and he returned to the same topic. In the course of his remarks he touched on the proposed raising of the school age. 'Lot o' voolery,' he snorted. 'Whatever be 'em thinkin' about? Doan't 'em know what'll happen? If they keeps childer at school till they be sixteen, more'n half on 'em'll be vair spoiled fore they do leave. Childer wants to be broke to work young, like colts. Work never hurt I, and I never knowed it hurt nobody.'

I make no comment as to whether his prophecy will be correct or not. That his remarks will be regarded as a foul slander on rural youth, I have no doubt, but I would point out that the speaker had lived for eighty years in a rural district, and therefore presumably was qualified to give his opinion. I sometimes wonder if the people in Whitehall are so well qualified.

Apart from the effects of the depression which was more

and more rapidly creeping over the countryside, the actual farming itself lacked romance and charm at this date as compared to pre-War days. Agriculture was becoming mechanized. The horse was disappearing from the landscape, and giving place to the hideous tractor. I did not purchase one of these implements until our old portable steam engine came to the point in its long and dignified career when the cost of adequate repairs was prohibitive.

When the tractor arrived the men viewed it with scorn. Its size as compared with the huge bulk of the steam engine made it appear as a toy. We arranged to thresh with it a day or two after its arrival, and the feeder of the threshing machine said 'as 'ow 'ee wor gwaine to feed zo as to bring a little pooper like that up all standin''.

Next morning, when all was ready, I let in the friction clutch on the pulley wheel of the tractor, and when the hum of the threshing machine had reached its correct note, I waved my arm to the feeder to begin. He did so, and the rich hum of the thresher died away as the machine slowed down. The men's faces were triumphant, whilst mine was the reverse. However, I noticed that although the machine slowed down, the tractor maintained its speed, and therefore the clutch must have been slipping. I stopped the engine, studied the instruction book which had come with it, and tightened various nuts and springs on the clutch.

We started again, and despite the feeder's almost superhuman efforts, the tractor drove the thresher so fast that he was nearly shaken off his perch, and was forced to admit defeat.

But all the time, at the back of every one's mind, was the knowledge that things were very wrong with farming. Farmers generally spent less and less time and money in sport and pleasure, and what pleasures we did indulge in had lost their savour. In this I refer to the older men. The young generation, from eighteen to twenty-five, knew nothing about the tragedy in the background, and seemingly cared less. I had a friend stopping with me in the summer of 1927, and took him one afternoon to a tennis tournament in a nearby village. Ostensibly it was in aid of a new church organ or similar object, but in reality it was an excuse for the youth of the district to have a good time.

'But where's this agricultural depression you've been telling me about?' asked my friend, as he gazed at the array of cars and at the expensively garbed youthful throng on the tennis-courts.

'It's there all right, in the background,' I said. 'These kids don't know anything about it, but their parents do.'

We sat and listened to the chatter. Said one young damsel to another: 'My dear, a frightful thing's happened. My new racket's got a string gone. Just my luck. Whatever shall I do?'

'Well, you've got another with you, so you can manage,' replied her companion.

'But, my dear, I shan't be able to hit a ball with it. It's last year's.'

My friend looked at me, and we got up and moved away. 'Why in the devil don't their parents stop it?' he burst out. 'Why, dash it, my racket's five years old.'

'Don't ask me,' I said. 'It's beyond me. Pride chiefly, I expect.'

And then for five minutes he trumpeted his opinion of the farming population, and in most of it I felt bound to admit that he had reason.

But the depression was there. Farmers knew it, the

older labourers knew it, the banks knew it, and, above all, the merchant or middleman knew it. . . . And here I would like to put in a word in defence of the middleman. It has of late become the fashion to look on him as a parasite on the community. Farmers will, I think, agree with me that he is nothing of the kind. Personally, I have yet to find a middleman who is not performing a useful service for society, and all that he can earn thereby, in my opinion, he is entitled to keep. Moreover, for the past ten years right up till to-day, the agricultural merchant has carried, and is still carrying on his shoulders, a large proportion of British farming which, but for him, would collapse ignominiously. I have lived and farmed through those troublous times, and I am grateful enough to the merchant and middleman to say 'thank you' publicly for the help and courtesy which I have received from them.

By 1927, which, in addition to falling prices was a bad year for weather and crops, the rotten state of things in the agricultural world became more apparent. Here and there men who were regarded as wealthy by most folk went bankrupt. Many others who escaped this were forced to give up farming because of financial difficulties. Farmers were endeavouring to get their sons into jobs unconnected with farming when they left school. A bank or Government appointment was looked at as a safe haven for life. It became preferable to let one's son do anything or even to do nothing, rather than to finance him in any farming venture. The landlords suddenly discovered that there was grave danger that the farms becoming vacant would have to be farmed by themselves. No one seemed to want them. So rents went down a little, but they were still above the pre-War rate.

I was struggling on, barely keeping my head above water, when early in 1927 a neighbouring farmer invited me to go with him to the North of our country in order to inspect a new milking invention. I refer to the open-air system of milk production, which was then in its infancy. Five of us made the journey in a car, and discovered this invention in what may honestly be described as a 'Heath Robinson' condition. Quite frankly, we regarded it as a joke.

It was constructed of odd wheels and parts taken from derelict farm machinery. The milking cows were under-sized, and to our ideas not worth having in a dairy. But the thing worked, and the cows produced milk. We saw a man and a boy milk and feed seventy cows in two hours that afternoon with one of these outfits. In actual fact we saw, I think, three outfits at work. And above all, we met a man who was satisfied that his farming was prospering.

Still, we looked at his cattle, and remembered our own wealthy beasts at home. We thought of having one's milking dependent on the spark from one magneto: we considered the difficulties and discomforts of milking in the open air during bad weather, and while we were very interested, and said so, we went in to tea with the inventor, feeling that this sort of thing could never become a general practice.

Now all that afternoon we had been literally surrounded with milk, but when our host said to his daughter that we were ready for tea, she informed him that it would be necessary to wait for a few minutes as the milk had not yet come down from the fields. This afforded us great amusement, and one of the company informed the lady that had he known that they were short of milk he would have brought some down with him.

After tea we discussed costs and milk yields with our host, and after thanking him for a most interesting afternoon, we set off for home. It is interesting to record that of the five of us who visited that farm on that occasion, four are farming under that system to-day, and the fifth, I think, will soon be doing so.

Now all that year I kept worrying over this new idea, chiefly because my present methods were losing money, and something different had therefore to be done. I journeyed to the inventor's farm several times in company with my neighbour. In the June of that year the latter purchased an open-air outfit, and, as he farmed nearby, I was able to get many opportunities to study it.

He paid me a compliment one day by informing me that I wasn't quite such a silly fool as many young men of his acquaintance, in that I had realized for some time that farmers were living in a fool's paradise, and also that I had made some effort to put things right.

'What about it?' he continued. 'There's more to this outdoor business than appears at first sight.'

'I'm inclined to agree,' I replied, 'but I've tried so many things during the last few years, and found them disastrous, that I'm getting afraid to trust my own judgment.'

'Well,' he said, 'for your information, I'm going in for it whole hog. I've been milking over two hundred cows by hand in buildings, and it's got to stop. My pocket can't stand it.'

Now while it was a comparatively easy matter for a wealthy man of his type to change his whole system of farming, for a young man already at his last financial gasp to do so was a difficult matter. But the returns from the

1927 harvest and milk sales left me with no alternative. It was try something else or get out as a failure. True, it would be a leap into comparative darkness. I wondered if it would be a case of out of the frying pan into the fire. Still, the frying pan had become untenable, and as this new system of dairying seemed to show a possible way out, I decided to try it.

A. G. STREET, *Farmer's Glory* (1932)

V

CICELY'S DAIRY

By RICHARD JEFFERIES

A BLUE-PAINTED barrel churn stood by the door; young Aaron turned it in the morning, while the finches called in the plum trees, but now and then not all the strength of his sturdy shoulders nor patient hours of turning could 'fetch' the butter, for a witch had been busy.

Sometimes on entering the dairy in the familiar country way, you might find Cicely, now almost come to womanhood, at the cheese tub. As she bent over it her rounded arms, bare nearly to the shoulder, were laved in the white milk. It must have been from the dairy that Poppaea learned to bathe in milk, for Cicely's arms shone white and smooth, with the gleam of a perfect skin. But Mrs Luckett would never let her touch the salt, which will ruin the hands. Cicely, however, who would do something, turned the cheeses in the cheese-room alone. Taking one corner of the clean cloth in her teeth, in a second, by some dexterous sleight-of-hand, the heavy cheese was over, though ponderous enough to puzzle many a man, especially as it had to come over gently that the shape might not be injured.

She did it without the least perceptible exertion. At the moment of the turn, when the weight must have been felt, there was no knot of muscle visible on her arm. That is the difference; for

> When Ajax strives some rock's vast weight to throw

the muscles of the man's limb knot themselves and stand out in bold relief. The smooth contour of Cicely's arm never varied. Mrs Luckett, talking about cheese as we watched Cicely one morning, said people's taste had much altered; for she understood they were now fond of a foreign sort that was full of holes. The old saying was that bread should be full of holes, cheese should have none. Just then Hilary entered and completed the triad by adding that ale should make you see double.

So he called for the brown jug, and he and I had a glass. On my side of the jug stood a sportsman in breeches and gaiters, his gun presented, and ever in the act to fire: his dog pointed, and the birds were flying towards Hilary. Though rude in design the scene was true to nature and the times: from the buttons on the coat to the long barrel of the gun, the details were accurate and nothing improved to suit the artist's fancy. To me these old jugs and mugs and bowls have a deep and human interest, for you can seem to see and know the men who drank from them in the olden days.

Now a tall Worcester vase, with all its elegance and gilding, though it may be valued at £5000, lacks that sympathy, and may please the eye but does not touch the heart. For it has never shared in the jovial feast nor comforted the weary; the soul of man has never communicated to it some of its own subtle essence. But this hollow bowl whispers back the genial songs that were shouted over it a hundred years ago. On the ancient Grecian pottery, too, the hunter with his spear chases the boar or urges his hounds after the flying deer; the women are dancing, and you can almost hear the notes of the flute. These things were part of their daily life; these are no imaginary pictures of imaginary and impossible scenes: they are simply scenes in which every one then took part. So I think that the old English jugs and mugs and bowls are true art, with something of the antique classical spirit in them, for truly you can read the hearts of the folk for whom they were made. They have rendered the interpretation easy by writing their minds upon them: the motto, 'Prosperity to the flock', for instance, is a good one still; and 'Drink fair; don't swear', is yet a very pleasant and suitable admonition.

As I looked at the jug, the cat coughed under the table. 'Ah,' said Mrs Luckett, 'when the cat coughs, the cold goes through the house.' Hilary, returning to the subject of the cheese, said that the best was made when the herd grazed on old pastures: there was a pasture field of his which it was believed had been grazed for fully two hundred years. When he was a boy, the cheese folk made to keep at home for eating often became so hard that, unable to cut it, they were obliged to use a saw. Still longer ago, they used to despatch a special cheese to London in the road-waggon; it was made in thin vats (pronounced in the dairy 'vates'), was soft, and eaten with radishes. Another hard kind was oval-shaped, or like a pear; it was hung up in nets to mature, and traded to the West Indies.

RICHARD JEFFERIES, *Round About a Great Estate* (1880)

VI

COWMAN AND DAIRY

By T. HENNELL

THE farmer or cowman gets up at about half-past four in the summer, or six o'clock in the winter, and calls in the cows for milking. They are turned out immediately after and are milked again, as a rule, about four in the afternoon. Near Frome, in fine weather, the cows are milked in the fields; and I have heard that this is done in some other places.

The cowhouse or shippen, if it is of the old sort, is a long building which has a stone cobbled floor with a gutter down the middle and stalls with pairs of upright posts along either side, between which the cows are tethered. But these stone floors will not be seen much longer, for by Act of Parliament farmers must put down floors of concrete instead. On the sweet breath of the cows, the steady sound of crunching and the hiss of the milk into the pails, it is unnecessary to enlarge; no doubt the old style of hand-milking will be practised for many years to come, though the mechanical milker is used on very many farms, and though less pleasant to the imagination it is, one is told, not less acceptable to the cows.

By increased production price is often reduced, and thus things are made more difficult for the small producer. One farmer complained that a government instructor had taught him and his neighbours to get three gallons of milk a day where they formerly only got two; the result was that while feeding cost more they got no more money for their three gallons than formerly for two, the demand not having increased with the supply. 'Now if he had taught us to get only one gallon,' he concluded, 'there would only be enough milk for those that want it, and we should get a better profit than we do now!'

The large farmer is naturally inclined to consider his animals not as individuals, but as mere units of efficiency; but it is by no means so with those who have only a few, upon which their living depends. The poor people in Kerry used to give the cow first place before the hearth in their cabins; they kept them indoors not, as Arthur Young suggested, to save the manure, but because the warmth increased their yield. An Irish shepherd keeps his lambs, too, in the house at night, 'to save them', as he says, 'from the dogs'.

Few people have any idea of the extent to which domestic animals respond to personal care, nor what intimate under-standing of them is possessed by those whose lives are passed in tending them. To illustrate this I copy out the following note, made last year:

F. S. was anxious about a mare which was going to have a foal, and she dreamt one night that it had two foals, one a fine red fellow with three white legs and a white nose, and the other one a little tiny thing no bigger than a dog. There came a great black dog and carried off the big fellow and left the little one. The next morning she went out and there the two foals were, at the very spot in the Barn Meadow, between the ditch and the apple tree by the gate, exactly as she had dreamed of them, a big one and a little one. They reared the little one with a bottle, and it lived and was afterwards sold, but the big one fell sick and died after a fortnight. At many other times F. has dreamed of things which have happened, especially with animals she was rearing.

2-2

Dairywork has come to belong to factories instead of, as formerly, to the farmer's household: the whole day's milk being more often than not put through coolers and taken off in a lorry. But the old processes of skimming off the cream, churning, salting, and rolling the butter are too well known to justify an account here.

The separator has taken the place of the brass and earthenware pans or lead coolers, except in Devonshire and Cornwall, where clotted cream is made in the old way, by scalding over the fire. Several forms of churn are made; nowadays they are nearly always of the 'barrel' or 'end-over-end' types. The old upright or dash-churns, in which the work was done by means of a plunger, bored with holes and with a long handle, were made in the northern counties by some coopers who are still in business; but though a few of them are no doubt in existence still, they are long out of fashion and have been replaced by more modern types. As every one knows, a cool hand is an indispensable qualification of a good dairymaid, for pressing the buttermilk out of the butter, without making it heavy or greasy. In the north of Dartmoor this was not long ago a still more important gift: for the cream was put in a tub and churned *by hand*, the dairywoman's arm being plunged to the elbow. In the Science Museum at South Kensington there is a most elaborate engine for turning a barrel churn by gears from an immense spur wheel, the power having been supplied by a horse or bull.

Whatever may be the popular notion in the matter, good farm butter is better in colour, richer and more nourishing than factory butter; indeed it *tastes* of butter, which the hard, white stuff sold by grocers does not. It does not pay a farmer to 'blend' or adulterate his butter, but to make it of as good quality as possible. Butter, like flour, bread and meat, is devitalized and its wholesome nature destroyed, the more it is passed through mechanical processes.

A substitute has in the same way been found for farm-house cheese, in the form of a tough gelatinous matter wrapped in tinfoil; which, though it costs the customer as much, is more profitable to the shopkeeper. However, in spite of this competition, some of the better sorts have survived, while in Suffolk one may be fortunate enough to get excellent cream cheese, in place of the once famous flinty substance described by Bloomfield, made from 'three-times skimmed sky-blue', which, after defying all attempts to cut it with a knife, at last

> in the hog-trough rests in perfect spite,
> Too big to swallow, and too hard to bite.

Nowadays essence of rennet, for curdling the milk, is bought from the grocer, but the old way was to salt and dry the maws or vells of sucking calves and to keep them for a year before use, then making an infusion from them in water or whey, with the addition of lemon juice. Occasionally a decoction of the flower called 'yellow lady's bedstraw' was used as a substitute for rennet.

Cheeses of different kinds are produced partly by differences of pasture or feeding, but chiefly by the different states of the milk, or milk and cream, at the time of curdling: several 'meals' of milk being sometimes combined, the night's cream, for example, being added to the morning's whole milk. The curds were first separated from the whey by cloths and then packed into cheese tubs or chessarts, the cheese press being used to squeeze out the last of the whey. But the old wooden cheese presses, with stones weighing a couple of hundredweight, and the clumsy screw presses which succeeded them are long since done away with, and the whey is now pressed out of the cheese by a more simple and efficient system of weights and levers.

'Green cheeses' used to be coloured in Wiltshire with sage, marigold and parsley leaves, bruised and steeped overnight in milk; the leaves being sometimes left in the cheese. 'Double Gloucester', an excellent cheese, was painted outside, after salting and scraping, with a mixture of Indian red, or Spanish brown, and small beer; it was known by the 'blue coat' which in time appeared through the paint. Egg cheeses were made in the north of England, three or four yolks going to every pound of curd.

T. HENNELL, *Change in the Farm* (1934)

VII

A WINTER MORNING

By RICHARD JEFFERIES

THE pale beams of the waning moon still cast a shadow of the cottage when the labourer rises from his heavy sleep on a winter's morning. Often he huddles on his things and slips his feet into his thick 'water-tights'—which are stiff and hard, having been wet overnight—by no other light than this. If the household is comparatively well managed, however, he strikes a match, and his 'dip' shows at the window. But he generally prefers to save a candle, and clatters down the narrow steep stairs in the semi-darkness, takes a piece of bread and cheese, and steps forth into the sharp air. The cabbages in the garden he notes are covered with white frost, so is the grass in the fields, and the footpath is hard underfoot. In the furrows is a little ice—white because the water has shrunk from beneath it, leaving it hollow—and on the stile is a crust of rime, cold to the touch, which he brushes off in getting over. Overhead the sky is clear—cloudless but pale—and the stars, though not yet fading, have lost the brilliant glitter of midnight. Then, in all their glory, the idea of their globular shape is easily accepted; but in the morning, just as the dawn is breaking, the absence of glitter conveys the impression of flatness—circular rather than globular. But yonder, over the elms, above the cowpens, the great morning star has risen, shining far brighter, in proportion, than the moon; an intensely clear metallic light—like incandescent silver.

The shadows of the trees on the frosted ground are dull. As the footpath winds by the hedge the noise of his footstep startles the blackbird roosting in the bushes, and the bird bustles out and flies across the field. There is more rime on the posts and rails around the rickyard, and the thatch on the haystack is white with it in places. He draws out the broad hay-knife—a vast blade, wide at the handle, the edge gradually curving to a point—and then searches for the rubber or whetstone, stuck somewhere in the side of the rick. At the first sound of the stone upon the steel the cattle in the adjoining yards and sheds utter a few low 'moos', and there is a stir among them. Mounting the ladder he forces the knife with both hands into the hay, making a square cut which bends outwards, opening from the main mass till it appears on the point of parting and letting him fall with it to the ground. But long practice has taught him how to balance himself half on the ladder, half on the hay. Presently, with a truss unbound and loose on his head, he enters the yard, and passes from crib to crib, leaving a little here and a little there. For if he fills one first, there will be quarrelling among the cows, and besides, if the crib is too liberally filled, they will pull it out and tread it underfoot. The cattle that are in the sheds fattening for Christmas have cake as well, and this must be supplied in just proportion.

The hour of milking, which used to be pretty general everywhere, varies now in different places, to suit the necessities of the milk trade. The milk has, perhaps, to travel three or four miles to the railway station; near great towns, where some of the farmers deliver milk themselves from house to house, the cows are milked soon after noonday. What would their grandfathers have said to that?

But where the old customs have not much altered, the milker sits down in the morning to his cow with the stars still visible overhead, punching his hat well into her side— a hat well battered and thickly coated with grease, for the skin of the cow exudes an unctuous substance. This hat he keeps for the purpose. A couple of milking pails—they are of large size—form a heavy load when filled. The milker, as he walks back to the farmhouse, bends his head under the yoke—whence so many men are round-shouldered— and steps slowly with a peculiar swaying motion of the body, which slight swing prevents it from spilling.

Another man who has to be up while the moon casts a shadow is the carter, who must begin to feed his team very early in order to get them to eat sufficient. If the manger be over-filled they spill and waste it, and at the same time will not eat so much. This is tedious work. Then the lads come and polish up the harness, and so soon as it is well light get out to plough. The custom with the horses is to begin to work as soon as possible, but to strike off in the afternoon some time before the other men, the lads riding home astride. The strength of the carthorse has to be husbanded carefully, and the labour performed must be adjusted to it and to the food, i.e. fuel, consumed. To manage a large team of horses, so as to keep them in good condition, with glossy coats and willing step, and yet to get the maximum of work out of them, requires long experience and constant attention. The carter, therefore, is a man of much importance on a farm. If he is up to his duties, he is a most valuable servant; if he neglects them, he is a costly nuisance; not so much from his pay, but because of the hindrance and disorganization of the whole farm-work which such neglect entails.

Foggers and milkers, if their cottages are near at hand, having finished the first part of the day's work, can often go back home to breakfast, and, if they have a good woman in the cottage, find a fire and hot tea ready. The carter can rarely leave his horses for that, and therefore eats his breakfast in the stable; but then he has the advantage that up to the time of starting forth he is under cover. The fogger and milker, on the other hand, are often exposed to the most violent tempests. A gale of wind, accompanied with heavy rain, often reaches its climax just about the dawn. They find the soil saturated, and the step sinks into it—the furrows are full of water; the cow-yard, though drained, is a pool, no drain being capable of carrying it off quick enough. The thatch of the sheds drips continually; the haystack drips; the thatch of the stack, which has to be pulled off before the hay-knife can be used, is wet; the old decaying wood of the rails and gates is wet. They sit on the three-legged milking stool (whose rude workmanship has taken a rude polish from use) in a puddle; the hair of the cow, against which the head is placed, is wet; the wind blows the rain into the nape of the neck behind, the position being stooping. Staggering under the heavy yoke homewards, the boots sink deep into the slush and mire in the gateways, the weight carried sinking them well in. The teams do not usually work in very wet weather, and most of the outdoor work waits; but the cattle must be attended to, Sundays and holidays included. Even in summer it often happens that a thunderstorm bursts about that time of the morning. But in winter, when the rain is driven by a furious wind, when the lantern is blown out, and the fogger stumbles in pitchy darkness through mud and water, it would be difficult to imagine a condition of things which concentrates more discomfort.

If, as often happens, the man is far from home—perhaps he has walked a mile or two to work—of course he cannot change his clothes, or get near a fire, unless in the farmer's kitchen. In some places the kitchen is open to the men, and on Sundays, at all events, they get a breakfast free. But the kindly old habits are dying out before the hard-and-fast money system and the abiding effects of Unionism, which, even when not prominently displayed, causes a silent, sullen estrangement.

Shepherds, too, sometimes visit the fold very early in the morning, and in the lambing season may be said to be about both day and night. They come, however, under a different category from the rest of the men, because they have no regular hours, but are guided solely by the season and the work. A shepherd often takes his ease when other men are busily labouring. On the other hand, he is frequently anxiously engaged when they are sleeping. His sheep rule his life, and he has little to do with the artificial divisions of time.

Hedgers and ditchers often work by the piece, and so take their own time for meals; the ash woods, which are cut in the winter, are also usually thrown by the piece. Hedging and ditching, if done properly, is hard work, especially if there is any grubbing. Though the arms get warm from swinging the grub-axe or billhooks, or cleaning out the ditch and plastering and smoothing the side of the mound with the spade, yet feet and ankles are chilled by the water in the ditch. This is often dammed up and so kept back partially, but it generally forces its way through. The ditcher has a board to stand on; there is a hole through it, and a projecting stick attached, with which to drag it into position. But the soft soil allows the board to sink, and he often throws it aside as more encumbrance than use.

He has some small perquisites: he is allowed to carry home a bundle of wood or a log every night, and may gather up the remnants after the faggoting is finished. On the other hand, he cannot work in bad weather.

Other men come to the farm buildings to commence work about the time the carter has got his horses fed, groomed and harnessed, and after the fogger and milker have completed their early duties. If it is a frosty morning and the ground firm, so as to bear up a cart without poaching the soil too much, the manure is carried out into the fields. This is plain, straightforward labour, and cannot be looked upon as hard work. If the cattle want no further attention, the foggers and milkers turn their hands after breakfast to whatever may be going on. Some considerable time is taken up in slicing roots with the machine, or chaff-cutting —monotonous work of a simple character, and chiefly consisting in turning a handle.

The general hands—those who come on when the carter is ready, and who are usually young men not yet settled down to any particular branch—seem to get the best end of the stick. They do not begin so early in the morning by some time as the fogger, milker, carter or shepherd; consequently, if the cottage arrangements are tolerable, they can get a comfortable breakfast first. They have no anxieties or trouble whatever; the work may be hard in itself, but there is no particular hurry (in their estimation) and they do not distress themselves. They receive nearly the same wages as the others who have the care of valuable flocks, herds and horses; the difference is but a shilling or two, and, to make up for that, they do not work on Sundays. Now, the fogger must feed his cows, the carter his horses, the shepherd look to his sheep every day; consequently their extra wages are thoroughly well earned. The young labourer—who is simply a labourer, and professes no special branch—is, therefore, in a certain sense, the best off. He is rarely hired by the year—he prefers to be free, so that when harvest comes he may go where wages chance to be highest. He is an independent person, and full of youth, strength, and with little experience of life, is apt to be rough in his manners and not over civil. His wages too often go in liquor, but if such a young man keeps steady (and there are a few that do keep steady) he does very well indeed, having no family to maintain.

A set of men who work very hard are those who go with the steam-ploughing tackle. Their pay is so arranged as to depend in a measure on the number of acres they plough. They get the steam up as early as possible in the morning, and continue as late as they can at night. Just after the harvest, when the days are long, and, indeed, it is still summer, they work for extremely long hours. Their great difficulty lies in getting water. This must be continually fetched in carts, and, of course, requires a horse and man. These are not always forthcoming in the early morning, but they begin as soon as they can get water for the boiler, and do not stop till the work is finished or it is dark.

The women do not find much work in the fields during the winter. Now and then comes a day's employment with the threshing machine when the farmer wants a rick of corn threshed out. In pasture or dairy districts some of them go out into the meadows and spread the manure. They wear gaiters, and sometimes a kind of hood for the head. If done carefully, it is hard work for the arms—knocking the manure into small pieces by striking it with a fork swung to and fro smartly.

In the spring, when the great heaps of roots are opened—
having been protected all the winter by a layer of straw
and earth—it is necessary to trim them before they are
used. This is often done by a woman. She has a stool or
log of wood to sit on, and arranges a couple of sacks or
something of the kind, so as to form a screen and keep off
the bitter winds which are then so common—colder than
those of the winter proper. With a screen one side, the
heaps of roots the other, and the hedge on the third, she is
in some sense sheltered, and, taking her food with her, may
stay there the whole day long, quite alone in the solitude
of the broad, open, arable fields.

From a variety of causes, the number of women working
in the fields is much less than was formerly the case; thus
presenting precisely the reverse state of things to that
complained of in towns, where the clerks, etc., say that they
are undersold by female labour. The contrast is rather
curious. The price of women's labour has, too, risen; and
there does not appear to be any repugnance on their part
to field-work. Whether the conclusion is to be accepted
that there has been a diminution in the actual number of
women living in rural places, it is impossible to decide
with any accuracy. But there are signs that female labour
has drifted to the towns quite as much as male—especially
the younger girls. In some places it seems rare to see a
young girl working in the field (meaning in winter)—
those that are to be found are generally women well
advanced in life. Spring and summer work brings forth
more, but not nearly so many as used to be the case.

Although the work of the farm begins so soon in the
morning, it is, on the other hand, in the cold months, over
early. 'The night cometh when no man can work' was, one

would think, originally meant in reference to agricultural labour. It grows dusk before half-past four on a dull winter's day, and by five is almost, if not quite dark. Lanterns may be moving in the cow-yards and stables; but elsewhere all is quiet—the hedger and ditcher cannot see to strike his blow, the ploughs have ceased to move for some time, the labourer's workshop—the field—is not lighted by gas as the rooms of cities.

The shortness of the winter day is one of the primary reasons why, in accordance with ancient custom, wages are lowered at that time. In summer, on the contrary, the hours are long, and the pay high—which more than makes up for the winter reduction. A labourer who has any prudence can, in fact, do very well by putting by a portion of his extra summer wages for the winter; if he does not choose to exercise common sense, he cannot expect the farmer (or any manufacturer) to pay the same price for a little work and short time as for much work and long hours. Reviewing the work the labourer actually does in winter, it seems fair and just to state that the foggers, or milkers, i.e. the men who attend on cattle, the carters and the shepherds, work hard, continuously, and often in the face of the most inclement weather. The mere labourers, who, as previously remarked, are usually younger and single men, do not work so hard, nor so long. And when they are at it—whether turning the handle of a winnowing machine in a barn, cutting a hedge, spreading manure, or digging—it must be said that they do not put the energy into it of which their brawny arms are capable.

'The least work and the most money', however, is a maxim not confined to the agricultural labourer. Recently I had occasion to pass through a busy London street in the

West End where the macadam of the roadway was being picked up by some score of men, and, being full of the subject of labour, I watched the process. Using the right hand as a fulcrum and keeping it stationary, each navvy slowly lifted his pick with the left half-way up, about on a level with his waistcoat, when the point of the pick was barely two feet above the ground. He then let it fall—simply by its own weight—producing a tiny indentation such as might be caused by the kick of one's heel. It required about three such strokes, if they could be called strokes, to detach one single small stone. After that exhausting labour the man stood at ease for a few minutes, so that there were often three or four at once staring about them, while several others lounged against the wooden railing placed to keep vehicles back.

A more irritating spectacle it would be hard to imagine. Idle as much agricultural labour is, it is rarely so lazy as that. How contractors get their work done, if that is a sample, it is a puzzle to understand. The complaint of the poor character of the work performed by the agricultural labourer seems also true of other departments, where labour—pure and simple labour of thews and sinews—is concerned. The rich city merchant, who goes to his office daily, positively works harder, in spite of all his money. So do the shopmen and assistants behind their counters; so do the girls in drapers' shops, standing the whole day and far into the evening when, as just observed, the fields have been dark for hours; so, indeed, do most men and women who earn their bread by any other means than mere bodily strength.

But the cattlemen, carters, and shepherds, men with families and settled, often seem to take an interest in their charges, in the cows, horses or sheep: some of them are really industrious, deserving men. The worst feature of unionism is the lumping of all together, for where one man is hardly worth his salt, another is a good workman. It is strange that such men as this should choose to throw in their lot with so many who are idle—whom they must know to be idle—thus jeopardizing their own position for the sake of those who are not worth one-fifth the sacrifice the agricultural worker must be called upon to make in a strike. The hardworking carter or cattleman, according to the union theory, is to lose his pay, his cottage, his garden and get into bad odour with his employer, who previously trusted him, and was willing to give him assistance, in order that the day labourer, who has no responsibilities either of his own or his master's and who has already the best end of the stick, should enjoy still further opportunities for idleness.

RICHARD JEFFERIES, *Hodge and his Masters* (1880)

VIII

CORN-CARTING

By GEORGE BOURNE

THE works of farming go on almost as quietly as those of Nature herself. As I look from my window it occurs to me that in the last twenty hours some of the colours of the country have changed as by stealth. One field especially, which was grey tawny yesterday, and last week bright with corn, to-day shows dark violet and brown. The plough was at work there yesterday. Now and again a flash of harness glanced across the valley; now and again a far-off exhortation from the ploughman to his horses reached me. But this was only another natural sound, like that of the rooks following the new furrows. The thing was going on so quietly that I hardly noticed it as going on at all, and the change is almost surprising now.

In late August days, particularly, the transformations seem almost as if the weather had effected them. They take place mysteriously. The populations of corn-shocks silently make their appearance in the fields, and then by-and-by are gone, you hardly know how. Only, as they disappear, you are aware of some mushroom growth or other of a rick, which was not there within the hedgerow, when you passed in the morning. If you chance upon the rick when it is growing, with its builders atop of it, you may hear a rustling of dry sheaves, or a quiet murmur of country voices, but that is all; and the rather tired sound of the breeze in the elms and oaks of the near hedgerow is not more peaceful.

How much of this may be due to the close fitting of the work, in all its details, to the conditions of Nature herself, I do not know. Most work has to fit close, but the work of farms, including these harvest tasks, is a kind of soft treading in the footsteps of Nature, so that the charm is never broken. Deftness of handling, with good management, is what the whispering sheaves seem to ask for, and to get. Some knack goes with the carrying of the corn and the building of the rick; but there is even more of accumulated common sense in it, by which the harvesters do not so much force Nature's acquiescence as humour her to their will. By aid of stored-up experience, without clash or friction, steadily, swiftly, the rustling corn is spirited from the far corners of the field to the rick; and it does not sound or look like a very busy process, but like a leisurely one, until you examine it closely. And that is just the way with Nature's own processes, too.

By long practice the farmer whom I saw taking up his oats had become himself the most quiet but effective medium of the forces by which corn is harvested. He was seventy years old, and said he could not work so well as he used to; but the precious knack, and the more precious common sense, that he had at command, made the work go smoothly and look easy, like playing the fiddle. Perhaps a fifth of the field—not more—had been cleared when I found him there, keeping an eye on everything and leading the horse, as the waggon trundled along beside the rows of sheaves. The sheaves had been pulled over on to their sides beforehand, that their butts might be dry when they were lifted, and they lay in little heaps of six, ready for pitching into the waggon. Of course, everyone can picture the scene; the field ringed by its hedgerow, dark green against the pale stubble; the width of space and air, the long vistas of shocks, the farmer with his horse, and the waggon and the two other men, one standing on it to receive the corn tossed up to him by the other. But the nicety of their interacting efforts will bear speaking of. It was 'like clock-work'. Trudging easily beside the waggon, Charlie, the carter (good, capable, brown-armed man, with wide mouth and steady eyes), wasted no movements. As he thrust the pitchfork—which is a tool shapely as any natural growth— into the sheaves near their straw-band, and so raised them aloft two at a time, and turned them over into the waggon, his action went into circles rhythmical and flowing. In comparison his mate's movements in the waggon seemed a scramble, yet he was ready each time to receive the ad-ditions to his load, and there was more in his work than could be seen from the ground. But of that by-and-by. At the horse's head the farmer was watching, peering round from the near side where he stood to the man pitching on the off side, and at every third pitch, as the prong was withdrawn from the last two sheaves, 'Stand hard!' said the farmer, and the horse strained and the waggon moved forward to the next heap, where a 'Wo-o' stopped the horse again. 'Stand hard—Wo-o', in two notes, of which the second was a little the higher, this sound accompanied the waggon along the rows, and was as apt to the country as any repeated call of wood-pigeon or peewit. So it went all the afternoon, monotonous and pleasing. Necessity kept it alive and exact. The 'Wo-o', being addressed to the horse, never varied; nor did the 'stand hard' vary in pitch or tone-quality, for it had to reach the man in the waggon, as a warning to him of the movement which at once followed. Sometimes the words were altered to 'Stand tight', or 'Stand fast', but not the sound, which had a slight chanting ring in it, capable of suggesting caution, but had no loudness to disturb the quiet of the afternoon.

There came a short interruption of it, and it was like breaking a silence. In this interval I said something about the ever-renewed call of warning; and the farmer remarked, 'The old carter we used to have would never say it. Very dangerous for the man in the waggon, because it might go on unexpected, and overbalance him. I used to say to the others, "You've got more patience than I should have had at your age. After he'd served me that trick three or four times, I should have been down out of the waggon and punched his head."' Meanwhile, the other two had changed places, and Charlie, now standing up in the waggon, was fidgeting about with his belt. 'He've brought it all up in lumps, all round under my belt', I heard him say; and the other laughed, 'Hit 'im with your fist!' 'What is it?' I asked. The farmer answered, 'Emmet, or something, inside his shirt.'

Emmet, or whatever it was, Charlie had to endure it, for the afternoon's work might not be dislocated. Right away across the field the rick was a-building, and by now was some eight feet high. I admired how level they were keeping it on the top. Two men stood there taking the sheaves from a third who pitched them up with methodical prong action out of another waggon in which he was standing. But if Charlie, where we were, stopped to catch his emmet, those three out there would presently be hindered. It was necessary for the two sets of three to keep their respective halves of the work balanced; so on the waggon went, while Charlie's mate now wielded the pitchfork, saving time not by hurry, but by exercise of care. How?

Simply by depositing each sheaf the right way about, so that
Charlie had no need to turn them over. The ears must lie
inside, and it is the butt of the sheaf that projects over the
waggon. And this is no caprice, but necessity will have it
so. Though it looks a scrambling affair, and is, of course, a
very simple one, still this loading up of corn-sheaves is a
kind of primitive art, and it reaches down for its justifi-
cation among some of the pleasantest of natural facts.
Because the stalks of corn have chosen, such ages ago, to
grow as they do, and now make bunches of a certain shape
when tied together, there is one good way, and perhaps
only one, of piling sheaves on a waggon; and it is by
practising this one way that the harvesters can save their
load from falling asunder and bring it home. Therefore,
they work quietly, keeping hands and eyes busy, so that
by the time the other waggon by the rickside is empty
theirs may be coming up to it full.

Once there, a variation of the same primitive art comes
into play. And since this quiet efficiency of the harvesting
is my subject, I may hardly digress to tell how, when the
waggons were changing, the distracted Charlie, retiring
towards the hedge so as to be screened from the high road,
took off his shirt to hunt for his tormentor, and found not
an emmet, but a spider. Seen against the dark autumn
foliage his naked skin was white and very picturesque; it
had a classical look, in what was otherwise a Constable
landscape. That, however, is not to my point. On the other
hand, I may not quite omit the contribution the waggons
made to the gentle sounds of the work. They passed almost
noiselessly over the stubble, and pressed but shallow ruts
into the dry soil; but the light clatter of hubs on axles
filled in, like a row of asterisks just audible, the space

between the farmer's 'Stand hard' and 'Wo-o'. I do not know a more peaceful sound. The second waggon contributed a groan too, where a loose spoke creaked in the near fore wheel. This sound, I admit, ought not to have pleased, but I learnt that the old waggon had gone through sixty previous harvests, and must through many of them have rattled most melodiously to be able still to creak.

After about two hours of this all but soundless labour, the rick (to come at last to that) had grown surprisingly, and now they were tapering it off towards the top ridge. It was a job that the farmer chose to superintend, and I stood at his side. No longer could the man in the waggon pitch the sheaves high enough; but, of course, experience has long known the way of getting over this difficulty. In a niche left half-way up the rick, a young man stood with pitchfork, receiving the sheaves sent up from the waggon and hoisting them again to the men at the top. He did his best, but, as was remarked to me, he had no knack, and was wasting some time. He failed to catch the sheaves direct from the other man's prong to his own; in fact, he made no attempt to do so, but waited until they were laid in the niche; and then, when he raised them, as often as not they were the wrong end foremost for the men on top. A Board-school product, I was told, this youth was, who had come to farm-work from a brewery store, where he had chiefly learnt to smoke cigarettes. In a few minutes, and without a word from anybody, Charlie slipped into his place, and things went more easily. The farmer gave a few directions as to raking out the sides of the rick, and so on; Charlie had something to settle about corn for his horses; and so we turned, the farmer and myself, leaving the men to finish.

At the gate of the field I looked back. It was a striking transformation I saw, for I had watched it in detail without realizing how much was being done. But there was a rick sprung up, sudden as a mushroom in the night; and, save for two or three rows still standing, the population of sheaves was gone. It seemed as if it must have happened while I was not looking; there had been no more noise than I have described, and yet the field was all but empty.

GEORGE BOURNE, *Lucy Bettesworth* (1913)

IX

COLT-BREAKING

By A. G. STREET

SOME people say that successful men are lucky. It often seems so, but I think that they have a special genius, a flair if you like, for doing the right thing, which cannot be defined exactly. I know that my father had this gift in a marked degree. It was our general custom to break in a cart colt or two each season. I had watched this proceeding several times as a boy, and it had always happened all right. Shortly after I left school, we took a colt out one morning to break it. When I say we, there were the foreman, and three carters in charge of the business; I was there for education, and the 'organizer' was absent.

In this particular case it didn't happen according to plan. With much 'woaing' and many 'stand still, oots', the colt was hitched to a plough alongside an old steady mare. The carter took hold of the plough handles and away they started, or should have started, with a few plunges from the youngster. But that youngster refused to budge. The old mare went away on the word of command, but the colt stood fast. They coaxed him with 'Now then, little feller' and other endearments, to no purpose. They whacked him, they swore at him, they made horrible, sudden, weird noises and catcalls in his rear, but there he stood, hunched in sullen immobility. The old mare would look round at him with an inquiring eye as if to say: 'Come on, I can't stay here all day.' Gradually the men lost their tempers and became more cruel in their methods of persuasion, but it was no good. 'Scoatin' little devil,' said one of the carters. ''Ee do beat all. Blast ye. Now then, coom up, Vi'let, altogether.' Vi'let came up nobly, but the colt was not included in the altogether. He evidently disapproved of team work. He was as the cat who walked by himself, save that he didn't walk, but stood by himself. Verily, all places were alike to him, for he showed no desire to go anywhere.

Finally, the breaking was abandoned. 'I doan't like giein' up,' said the foreman, 'but I bain't goin' to have 'ee beat no more. Dang 'un. You can do anything wi' 'em if only they'll goo, but when they wun't goo at all, you be done like. The Guvnor'll create about this, though.' The horses were unhitched, and, just as the disconsolate procession was leaving the field, my father appeared. 'What are you coming away for?' he asked the carter who was leading the colt. ''Ee wun't goo, zur, nowhow.'

'Won't go? Then he must be made to. Come on, back you go.'

And back we all squelched to the scene of our failure. My father's manner seemed to infuse a feeling of briskness into the proceedings. During the preliminary hitching he gave everybody the impression that this was a trivial business which would soon be over. As his son I knew jolly well that I would never dare to stand still if he wanted me to go anywhere, and I began to be a bit sorry for the colt. I felt that he couldn't possibly realize what he was now up against. When all was ready my father gave one last vicious instruction to the carter. 'Now then, Tom, when he starts, let 'un go. If you holler woa, I'll sack you. I'll tell 'ee when to stop. Now then.'

I think everybody present hoped that the colt would

refuse to budge. I know I did, as I wanted to find out the way to overcome this difficulty, but I can remember feeling quite sure that my father would have a certain cure for it.

'Noo then, Vi'let, coom up,' said Tom. As before, Vi'let came up in great style, but her companion failed again. But this time he went one better than just standing still. He went backwards a bit and sat down heavily.

Now a cart colt weighs nearly a ton, so if you can imagine a very fat man about twenty stone sitting down in a chair with a bump upon the point of a long sharp tin-tack, you will get some idea of what happened. There are lots of spiky things on an iron plough, and the colt sat down fairly on one of them (the drail pin is its correct name) and ran the point some three inches into his ham.

He didn't sit for long. No, by golly, he was up, and away with Vi'let doing her best to keep up, and Tom hanging on to the handles for dear life. The other men ran alongside over the rough ground in a stiff, scrambling, awkward gait—one's knees do not bend easily for running at sixty or thereabouts—whilst my father gallumphed along behind in like manner, giving tongue with hunting calls to cheer on the horses. 'Keep 'em going Tom,' he puffed. 'Don't let 'un stop on his own. He must go till we want him to stop.' And they kept him at it until he was a lather all over, and afterwards he was very little trouble. He was christened 'Squatter', and carried the mark of his squat all his life, as although he was a bright bay in colour, a small patch of white hairs grew over the wound in his ham.

Having demonstrated how easy it was to make a stubborn colt go, my father lectured the men on the imbecility of hitching off a colt before conquering it, and set off for another part of the farm to wake up somebody else. I stayed behind. The men's comments were much the same as my own would have been. 'Guvnor, 'ee do take all the credit for thic young vooil runnin' thic pint in his backside. Why hadn' er bin yer at the beginnin' and showed us how to do it? I 'low that 'ud a beat 'un. But there, things do allus goo right fer 'ee somehow.'

A. G. STREET, *Farmer's Glory* (1932)

X

THE SHEARER

By ADRIAN BELL

F ARTHING GRANGE was certainly an anachronism. It was an 'on-and-on' place. William used to have an old man to shear his sheep by hand, because he had been employed by his father always to help shear the flock: he was a good shearer and while he continued to go on working William would go on having his sheep done by hand. There had been others, but they had died or given up work, and Trimble was the only one left. So the shearing took longer, though the shepherd helped. Between them they did the whole flock. Trimble could shear thirty a day.

He was old but little abated in vigour, or he could not have caught and held a sheep while he clipped it. He spoke of the long hours of work when he was a boy and how his shoulders used to ache at the end of a day's shearing. It had meant at least two season's apprenticeship at a few shillings a week. It was considerable trouble to the old hands to teach a young one to shear; not only did the sheep have to be 'bellied out' for him (i.e. the wool clipped from the belly which was the trickiest part of the work, because the wool was thinner and the skin looser, and loose skin easily dragged into the shears and got cut), but he had to have an eye kept on him all the while. He was there to be shouted at for any mistakes, to be sent on errands, to fetch and carry for any who wanted.

Then too, he had to have his shears sharpened for him: the sharpening of the shears being highly skilled work—

more so than sharpening a scythe. The shepherd of
Farthing Grange himself admitted to being an indifferent
hand at the job.

'You'd never get one of the young 'uns to learn this
trade to-day,' said Trimble. 'They'd not have the patience.
Don't blame 'em neither: that's hard work and little hang
to it.'

Though he would not admit that the machine was
superior. 'You've got to have someone to turn it, and
there's nothing'll cut a sheep quicker if you aren't careful; as
soon as that drag the least bit. Stands to reason, them
knives are going such a rate. These things'—he held up the
hand shears—'you've got more management over them.'
He meant he had.

He and the shepherd had known each other as young
men; and while they worked they talked of old times.
Work and talk, the shearing was a spectacle that would be
a bit shocking to civilized sensibilities. A boarded platform
lay in the cart-lodge, raised slightly off the ground. The
whole was hurdled in, and divided inside by another row
of hurdles. At the back were penned the sheep to be
sheared. In the front the two men worked, covered with
grease and dung, each bent and involved with the limbs of
a sheep in something of a wrestler's attitude.

Every now and then, the sheep one of them held would
give a struggle to get free, and Trimble or the shepherd
would interrupt his reminiscence to swear at it.

'You silly old b——, d'you want to get cut?'

'Well, that girl she said to me, "Will you come to
Stambury with me Saturday morning?" Seeing as that
was bad weather, master let me go. She said, "I've got a
cheque and do you get the money for it for me." So we

went there in the bus ('that was a horse bus them days', he added for my benefit), and I said, "Give us the cheque." So I took it and got the money for it, and she give me a quid for doing that for her, and then we went and enjoyed ourselves.'

'She opened her heart then—if she gave you a quid,' I said.

'Ah, Mister, that was money easy come by, you see.' And they both laughed. 'She was a sportive young woman. But that didn't concern me how she earned her living. She always acted well by me.'

They went on working, taking a drink from the bottle provided by Master William after finishing a sheep, catching another and settling down to it again. And when they had got well into the fresh work the subject of the girls they had known started up again, and they would gloat anew over the looks of this one and the sportive ways of that one.

And the helpless, grandmotherly-looking sheep lolled in their arms, while the shears rang faintly with every snip and the muck-matted fleece rolled back. One gathered that that old life had not been all hard work at a few shillings a week. At least there had been pleasures enough (if not of a front-room decorum) to kindle at a distance this lively gossip.

Something of the old tiger would wake in Trimble. He had walked eight miles to work in the old days, arriving by six in the mornings, and still had had energy to spare for the making of these memories. He could not shear so many sheep in a day as he had been able to do; but his hand was still sensitive and sure with the shears, cutting crisply, carefully, making haste slowly. At the last snip he would

rise and stretch: 'There, you can go now.' The sheep
would remain in its position for a moment, dazed, then
writhe to its feet and leap away. Then he would slowly
enwrap and parcel up the fleece, compressing it with his
knee, weigh it in his hand, saying, 'There, that's a good
fleece', give it to us to handle, judge the weight of it once
more, then toss it up on to the heap in the wagon.

Then with sudden quivering energy, and shouting at me
as though I were deaf, he put his crook into my hand:
'There—that's a nice-made tool—feel the way it handle.'

It felt light and strong.

'That's a hand-made one (still shouting): I got it from
an old man in Bedfordshire when I went there when I was
young. Them you get nowadays are too heavy, they ain't
no good. Why I've had a sheep pull the crook right out.
This here wouldn't never give, none the more for being
light.'

'That's a tidy tool,' admitted the shepherd.

'The man that made that—' Trimble laughed. 'I see
him mending his watch once with a four-pound hammer.'

He had gone into Bedfordshire and then into Berkshire.
There he had collected a mythological history.

'Ah, that's a wonderful part of the country where I was—
they were digging there and they'd found some of them
Roman pavements that Cromwell knocked about. And
there was great stones set up on end (monoliths) what
they stood behind in them old days to fire off their blunder-
busses.'

That same day, I believe it was, I went to a country
house to tea. It stood secluded among its lawns and flowers;
and in the middle of the garden was a thatched building.
There were one or two looms inside, and here the daughter

of the house did hand-weaving. Not only did she weave, but took the wool from the fleece, washed it, dyed and spun it. She was at the moment out gathering young walnut leaves which made a golden-brown dye, and hanging in the sun outside the door were skeins dyed and drying. In one of the looms was a half-finished fabric in the soft and living colours of these vegetable dyes. The building was light and airy and gay with the woven cloth: there was that slight disorder of work in progress.

Then we had tea in a drawing-room, also light and airy with that indefinable optimism of a modern house. The talk was of the technicalities of hand-weaving, of gardens, of summer holidays.

And then I thought of Trimble and the shepherd shearing the sheep in the cart-lodge. They were still at it, rolling back the muck-matted wool, exchanging bawdy reminiscences.

And here we were—from the beginning to the end of the process. The skirt the girl was wearing she had woven herself, having first washed and dyed and spun the wool. Not only wool had been washed and fined and tinted and woven, but the texture of life had changed with it from Trimble to this flowered parlour. And the way we could be at ease with one another, with our knowledge of the gradations of pleasantness in things to be discussed, to be lightly skirted round, to be avoided. It was present to me in the light of Trimble's conversation as a subtly tinted and woven fabric; though as a rule one never even thought of it, knowing it all by instinct, so experienced were we in our end of the textile process.

I remembered Trimble's shouting at me to take the crook and feel what a handy tool that was; the vehemence of it

in his hand. Where now was that force? Driving the hand-loom?

Yet again a certain droop about the old man at the end of all that, as he started to walk home after his work—a sort of 'on-and-on' look.

'He go home early of a Saturday now,' the shepherd said to me. 'He lost his missus last spring and he have to look after himself now.'

A picture of him doing his week-end shopping; doing meek household things like putting on a kettle and washing up. No, I could not see it.

ADRIAN BELL, *By-Road* (1937)

XI

RURAL TECHNIQUE

By GEORGE BOURNE

TO the labourer already mentioned—that connoisseur of tools to whom spadefuls of earth are as words to the author, though unlike the author he never counts them—we are indebted for further evidence of the nice perceptive powers that a man must acquire for effective digging. The evidence, too, brings us a little nearer to the 'points' in which the fitness, and perhaps the beauty, of spades and shovels should be looked for. The old man was talking of a spade that had been provided for him in somebody's garden: ''Tis a spade!' he jeered. 'I expect they just sent to a shop for a "spade", and they got one! no mistake. Long, and straight, and heavy.... Now this little spade here', and he lifted the nearly new one he was using, 'it's a very nice little spade. I chose'n myself, out o' twenty or more they showed me at the shop. But he's too thick. He wants usin' in sharp sand for a week or two, to make 'n thinner; and that 'd wear off his sharp corners too, so's he'd enter the ground better. A spade's never no good till the corners is wore off. Same with a shovel. These navvies, when they buys a new shovel, very often they'll take 'n to the blacksmith's straight away, to have the corners chipped off. A blacksmith 'll do that for ye for nothin'—well, with his hard chisels it don't take 'n no time. And then just rub the corners smooth with a file....'

A more mysterious defect in this otherwise 'nice little spade' seemed to be beyond correction, as it was also beyond the power of an inexperienced eye to discern. 'It hadn't got quite a nice lift to it.' Observing how the tree or handle, where it curved down taperingly into the iron socket, was much straighter than that of a shovel which stood near, the amateur supposed that it was there that the fault lay. But he was quite wrong. In that respect the tool was all that a spade should be. ''Tis here in the blade. 'Ten't quite hollow enough for liftin' the earth. Still, 'tis a purty little spade.'

Groping thus to the truth of the matter, we may get further light on it by another consideration. We shall see how a scythe is fashioned to facilitate one definite movement, always in the same direction from right to left.* (The work of a gang of mowers is like drill, every man's part fitting in with his neighbour's, so that it would be impossible for any one of them to be left-handed.) And we have seen that an axe, by slightest alteration of the shaft, may be fitted to either hand, but once fitted to that, cannot be changed to the other. And now in spades and shovels we reach the other extreme; from the symmetry of these tools the possibility is manifest of shifting them from hand to hand, indifferently. It is a possibility which suggests that 'right-handedness', dexterity, may be dispensed with, or that the untrained gaucherie of an amateur may suffice. Instead of the strict handling that has shaped the scythe, we have with tools of this family a semblance of freedom too haphazard to have warped their balance into a specialized beauty.

Fortunately, there are other symmetrical tools, more familiar to the book-learned, to warn us against a false conclusion here. The skill necessary for using a steel pen or a dinner knife with one hand is commonly too exigent

* In Chapter XII.

to allow of its being acquired by the other, and the same truth holds good of shovels and spades and 'spuds'. If strength were all there is in it, one hand should be as ready for digging as the other; but the much-quoted labourer confesses, 'With a shovel I can only use it one way—with my left hand down towards the ground. But that's the left-handed way. If you puts me on to t' t'other way, all I can do is to move a little sand or anything like that, what's on the level. I en't no good that way.' 'No good', because in this man's estimation the little he can do does not amount to shovelling. To see what shovelling may be, one should watch navvies excavating for a sewer. As the narrow trench deepens, you lose sight of the men, but the shovel-fuls of earth come flying up orderly as ever on to the growing heaps at the side, two feet, three, four, five feet above the men's heads, never missing, never falling back nor , thrown too far. This is the sort of shovelling that the old labouring man means he can only do in 'the left-handed way'.

Put side by side, a spade and a shovel exhibit differences as significant as is their family likeness. They are as cousins. Sprung obviously from the same ancestry, each has diverged from the original in its own way, and with a reason for every modification. The reason, moreover, is the same as that which has fixed the shape of scythes, namely, to facilitate a difficult technical action. Nor is the type of shovel or spade any longer uncertain, albeit there are varieties of it. In the hands of generations of skilful labourers either tool has found its necessary definite form: the 'tree' tapering not without grace into the appointed curve of the iron; the blade wide and thin and shapely. And the type is so nearly perfect that the predilections of individual workmen may be ignored. They are too insignificant to be worth the manufacturer's attention. If our old labourer's spade had not quite a nice lift, yet it was a pretty little spade. And it had been made in America—at Chicago—stamped out with thousands more which were all fit and saleable, because all conformed to the unchangeable type towards which skill was striving before America had been heard of. It is hard to conceive a stronger proof of the existence of technique in shovelling and digging.

Of the technique which goes with hoeing the evidence is delightfully different. Spades may be best made at Chicago or at Birmingham, because the unwieldy iron and steel of them can be more finely forged by steam-hammers than by the village smith. But a hoe, being smaller, lighter, altogether more manageable, may be made by any blacksmith worth his salt. Consequently, although machine-made hoes are to be had cheap at any ironmonger's shop, the hand-made article holds its own in the market. For it would appear that a hoe is a more delicate instrument than a casual observer might suppose. For instance, the tool with which one man may do excellent work does not always suit another equally capable man, even on the same soil, until the adjustment of the handle in the socket has been altered. The soil, again, may necessitate a more radical change in the tool, beyond the hoer's power to effect; and this is where the local smith comes in, providing the hoe generally found most serviceable in his district. Not many years ago the West-Surrey labourer in want of a good hoe preferred one made by a certain blacksmith in Farnham, who knew better than can be known at Birmingham what was likely to be useful in his district. For wearing thin and true, and for convenient 'set' at the neck, this man's hoes in his best days could not be surpassed; but at the present

time the really desirable hoes for the same country come
from a smithy at Milford, near Godalming. And these are
so generally approved that farmers for miles round lay in
a stock of them to sell to their men, who, veritable con-
noisseurs, will sooner pay their employer for a Milford hoe
than go to a shop for a less useful though perhaps a cheaper
tool. Yet near Aldershot, and therefore practically in the
same neighbourhood, there are places where the Milford
hoe is found unsuitable to certain peculiarities of the soil,
and in these places the preferred pattern is one obtained at
Guildford. In view of all this, it cannot be necessary to
insist further upon the fineness of the technique of hoeing.
The fact that businesses thrive by supplying its demands
places its existence beyond a doubt. Actually there is
money in the recognition of it.

Indeed, in these local reputations for the make of certain
tools we tap another source of evidence, if more evidence
were needed, of the great technical accomplishments of the
labouring folk. Though less often now than of old, yet still
in sequestered villages, in workshops never heard of by
technical educators, good workmen win, not to publicity
perhaps, but to a curious fame amongst other working-
men, for their known ability in making beautiful or fit tools.
The present writer remembers a blacksmith in a village
too small to afford the man more than half a living, who
earned the other half by 'lining' or repointing with steel the
pickaxes and digging-forks brought to him by outside
appreciators. And we may recall the noted Pyecombe
crooks, mentioned by Sir Arthur Conan Doyle in *Rodney
Stone*. At one time, no South-Down shepherd felt himself
properly equipped for his work without a crook from the
Pyecombe smithy. Of course no one needs convincing that

a shepherd's work is full of minute technicalities—we have
read about them in Mr Hardy's amongst other books: but
the tale of human struggle and human skill suggested by a
Pyecombe crook, polished bright as silver for a good reason,
is one that would surpass all the art of fiction to tell. The
temptation is great to go on and speak of a family of smiths,
in a village no one ever heard of out of Surrey, whose edged-
tools—axes, chisels, planes—were coveted thirty years
ago by all wheelwrights and carpenters for miles round:
or of a wheelwright not so very far from the same village,
whose waggons to-day are in demand from Woking to the
Isle of Wight.

Without, however, wandering so far from the peasant
labourer, mention may yet be made of other essentially
rustic occupations that have their full measure of mystery.
Not to speak of sawyers who have almost disappeared
before the steam saw—for their exhausting labour in
couples impelled them to get drunk singly, and too often
on alternate days, to the unbearable annoyance of their
employers; or of threshers, whose winter employment has
made way for the charms of the steam threshing machine;
or of thatchers, or harvesters, or brickmakers, or quarry-
men, there are the 'hedgers and ditchers', whose work is
not quite so simple as might be thought. Only the other
day a farmer was complaining that, though he could find
three month's work for a man at hedging and ditching,
he could not find a man able to do the work, which, therefore, would have to be left undone. Again, there are the
copse-cutters, too interesting to be quite passed over.
According to an old farm-hand, 'There's a great deal of
art in copsin'. You gets so much a hundred for everything
you can save; so a man got to keep his eye on what he got

in his hand, to see what he can make of it. There's poles, and bow-shores, and shackles' (listen to the technical words—they relate to hurdle-making and sheep-folding), 'and rods, and pea-sticks—everything before the bavin comes; and bavin is the last. You gets so much a hundred for 'em all, and if a man don't make the most of 'em, he may soon throw away a day's earnin'.'

GEORGE BOURNE, *Lucy Bettesworth* (1913)

XII

SCYTHES

By GEORGE BOURNE

THE scythe is as a book—a book composed entirely out of doors by the English peasantry—in which, if one could read, one would learn much of their uneventful history, or, at any rate, would find much of their character recorded. One of these recent June days that truth was brought home to me by the talk of a man mowing under some old orchard trees. For he spoke of his scythe eagerly, proudly; so that it was plain to see how there must be an interaction between the tool and the man using it, good for both; the man's interest being first animated and his faculties sharpened by the exactions of the scythe, and then the scythe being gradually improved to meet the demands of the man's heightened skill.

It was one, Bridger, a Wiltshire man—whose rapid dialect I cannot reproduce nor always follow—who permitted me to handle and examine his scythe. Near the cranked end of the blade there was a tiny hole which excited my curiosity. 'That's for a grass-wire,' I was told. 'You drive a staple into the butt of the shaft and stretch a wire from it to this hole to keep the grass from cloggin' in the crank when you are mowing field-grass.'

Bridger's cramped old hands were itching, I could see, to get hold of the scythe again; but I still held it, and he went on to tell how all scythes are stamped on the back with T or W, or M, 'for the day of the week'. I turned the thing over—long, true, keen-edged, bright. Just within the backbone, on the under side, there ran a deep groove the whole length of the blade for some mysterious reason; and stamped in this groove was a legend half clogged with dirt. Between us we gradually made this out to be 'James Russell Wells'. Who was he? The maker, Bridger guessed, but did not know. Nearer the point the words 'Best Crown' could be deciphered; and that was all I could see. But Bridger seemed discontented with me, and with the scythe too, until presently, 'What's that?' he said. 'That's a T, en't it, up there?' He pointed to the part where the crank broadens to the blade, and there, sure enough, was a small letter T. 'That's for Tuesday or Thursday,' he said. 'That's the day o' the week when she was made. They be all stamped like that, to show what day o' the week they was made on.' But why? ''Tis something to do with the fire—the heat, you know. The fires en't so good the beginning of the week, but by about Thursday—Wednesday or Thursday'—by then, according to Mr Bridger, the cutler's heat is at its best. Wherefore, 'if you buy a scythe with W stamped on it, for Wednesday, or F for Friday—that's another good day—it will be a middling good scythe.' But if the letter is M—well, Bridger shook his head at the thought of M and a Monday's scythe.

I looked at the wedges that fix the shaft into the socket, wondering and asking if individual mowers found it necessary or possible to adjust the blade differently, as in the case of hoes, each man according to his own needs. But Bridger did not understand.

'You takes 'em to the blacksmith', he said, 'and they sets 'em down a little at the crank. The blacksmith knows about what is wanted.'

'Then you don't alter them for yourself by the wedges?'

'No—well—but the blacksmith knows near the matter. But 'tis in the nibs.' He took the tool back at last into his own possession, and resting the lower nib on his stretched-out finger showed how the scythe hung balanced there with its blade level with the grass. 'You got to be careful how you put the nibs on.' Turn this lower one but a shade upwards, and as you grasp it the blade points up into the air, but a turn ever so little downwards sends the point digging viciously into the ground.

Stooping suddenly to pick up his whetstone, Bridger planted the point of the blade on the ground and began vigorously sharpening. 'If you don't know how to sharp a scythe,' he remarked, 'you en't no good with 'n.' So I watched, noting, what could be judged, too, from the sound, how considerable and how regular a pressure went into each stroke of the whetstone. 'Some sharps 'em like this,' he drew the stone down, but only once, at an angle of perhaps twenty degrees with the edge, 'but the edge don't last two minutes that way.' The proper method, he seemed to say, is to keep the stone flat, with alternate strokes on back and front. He talked and showed, then suddenly stood up and began cutting. Clean and sweet the blade went through the grass, close to the ground, and the fascinating 'swish' of its progress seemed part of the tune of summer.

It was what Bridger called a 'light' rather than an 'easy' cut, there under the trees, where the grass had gone 'wilty' and pale, with poor seed. But though in long and dense 'field-grass' the cutting is easier, in the sense of being more complete and clean, I understood from Bridger that the mere pulling is heavy work. A seven-pound scythe and a weight of grass: clearly to keep lifting this all day long a man must be both skilful and fit. And I think it is because of this more than for any other reason that scythes seem to have such a charm about them. They suggest lovely weather; yes, and strong, quiet men, too, who in the practice of their craft must have attained something of the dignity of artists. And did not some vague art of living, simple but sincere, ripen among our English husbandmen, as age after age they whetted their skill by the use of scythes?

I look upon Bridger as one of the products of that art of living, and he is well worth looking at. Seventy years old, he is large, thick, strong, active, skilful. The sweat stood, as he talked to me, a drop or two on each eyebrow; his keen old eyes gleamed shrewd and kindly; the brick-dust colour of his cheeks was most wholesome. He took off his hat, and it was a massive head that showed; all but bald, and flattish on the top, but with a fringe of silky silver-grey hair, inclined to be curly over the nape. A handsome head; a tough, kindly, really grand specimen of an Englishman, whom all people who know him cordially like.

In the making of this man his scythe played its conspicuous part. And now that scythes are no doubt properly going out of date, one feels anxious to know whether the mowing machines, by which they are being superseded, are as good for our crop of Englishmen as they are for our hay crops. If the machine is likely to encourage skill and simple pride in the man who sits on it, and to keep him vigorous and genial and attentive, then, as we grow used to it, it will take its place in our affection, and we may even think it beautiful. All that, however, is for the future. Meanwhile, no such doubt exists with regard to the other tool; the scythe has justified itself, and deserves well all the admiration bestowed upon it.

GEORGE BOURNE, *Lucy Bettesworth* (1913)

XIII

STACKING

By ADRIAN BELL

I REMEMBER a windy June day when they were putting up a stack in a rather exposed position. Hunnable, Russiter, and one or two of the younger men were at it. In this the old fellows took charge as a matter of course. It was they who judged the amount of hay in the field; the size of stack-bottom to be stepped out and strawed. Russiter, a little grey man whose face had the vigorous eccentricity of an oak root, was stacker. Hunnable loaded the waggons to two young men's pitching.

The wind, that so refreshed the day, blew withered flowers and leaves into the stackers' faces. Beside the stack stood a large elm, and the noise of it was like the sea. I noticed a wagtail under it, about on a level with the men on the stack, neither flying nor settled, but holding itself still on the air with flickering wings. He gave a sense of speed to things.

Unloading hay is a dead-heavy job. The forkfuls at the bottom of the waggon get compressed and entangled, and as the unloader lifts one, with others probably hanging to it, he is smothered in a dusty shower that falls into his shirt, and collects round his waistbelt to prick him as he moves.

It is wonderful how much stuff (on the half-loaded waggon it almost looks like water in overflow) can be built into clean lines and angles. The result was symmetrical, it looked to have been done easily; but in fact the whole day long Russiter was in a state of anxiety, which showed itself by an unusual silence.

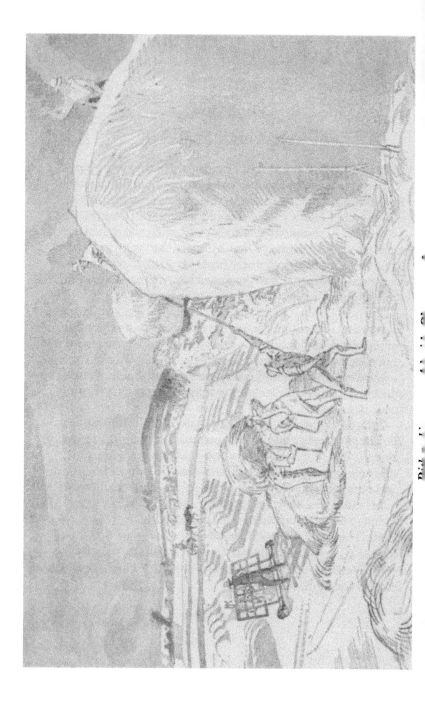

Birkenhead Ironworks, from the River Mersey

After a load had been flung off, and the others sank down on the stack to wait for the next, to chat and chew clover stalks, Russiter would clamber down the ladder and look at the stack from a distance, head on one side, to view his work as a whole. Then he would come and be pushing and prodding at the corners with a pitchfork till it was time for him to start stacking the next load.

If he spoke it was to the man who drove the waggon; asking him minute information as to the hay-cock topography of the field, whose latter half was hidden from us by a dip in the ground.

'They've left two rows round the hedge? How many double rows across to a load?' etc., etc. He was calculating all the time.

At one interval, after a drink, he did confide to me, 'I've stacked every harvest for forty years. I've not had a stack fall yet. But this is a rum corner for a stack with the wind blowing like that is to-day.'

This was a relic of old work. Russiter was concerned for his personal reputation. Hunnable loaded giant loads to perfection automatically, treading out upon their corners with assurance, thinking all the time probably about his bees. For the others, younger men, who were neither van drivers, budders, grafters, nor tractor men, it was but a relic. Such an occasion depended for its heartening on the wit and reminiscence of Russiter, who, on account of this wind, was silent. If they thought, it was in terms of hay sweeps and elevators for lightening the task; things which had been promised, but which had not arrived in time for the first stack.

A load came to the stack's side; the driver tied the trace-horse with its head to the back of the load (no more were to be fetched that day). 'So's that'll eat a little and then there won't be so much to unload,' he said.

They laughed; but despite cheerfulness on the surface, there was an undercurrent of tiredness.

The load was all uphill work: the stack was raised by now above it. At last the last forkful was pitched out. The man shook himself: then sat for a few minutes on the rail of the waggon resting; gazing at a myriad of earwigs that hustled to and fro on the floor among the chaff.

He said, 'If someone was to come along and give me a sovereign for every old earwig in this waggon....'

That being too unlikely a vision, 'Or even', he conceded, 'if anyone was to give me a shilling for every one I killed.' He prodded at them with his hay-fork.

It grew shadowy, with less wind. The cloth was laid over the stack; and the long ladder substituted for the short one to enable the men to come down.

There it stood against the sky, pointing sharply up high above the stack, like a rhetorical finger summoning to next day's work.

The next day was Sunday, though, and the wind got up again. The stack was not far from the cottage in which we were staying. I saw the cloth straining against the blocks to which it was fastened, bellying like a great sail. They were jumped up and down, and the surface of the stack on which the wind lay was ruffled up. Russiter standing in church must have seen all this going on in his mind's eye as plainly as I did. He came hurrying along, black suit and bowler, and began wrestling with the ropes. I went out to help him, and by one hanging on and the other tying, we managed to get them fixed to heavier pieces—lengths sawn for gate-posts, anything that lay handy.

Then he took a fork and began prodding at the corner of the stack again.

ADRIAN BELL, *By-Road* (1937)

XIV

HARVESTING IN THE OLD STYLE

By T. HENNELL

IN most parts of England reaping with sickles has been given up since about 1870, but this work is still to be seen in some parts of Scotland and Ireland. The sickle is a distinct tool from the broad and smooth-edged fagging-hook, which is still used for many jobs and for a time took its place in the harvest fields of most parts of England before reaping machines became common. Its blade is in the form of a continuous curve, ending in a point several inches beyond the line of the handle; this point is not sharpened and serves to divide the straws of the standing corn. An inch or so from the point the edge is sharp and serrated, nicks being filed along the under side of the blade (which is somewhat concave), in such a way that they radiate, as it were, from the 'heel' of the blade. About half a dozen patterns of sickle are still made, or at any rate listed by the large firms of tool-makers in Sheffield; those which still survive are mostly coarser-toothed and rather smaller than the sickles which were formerly used in England. It may be added that the sickle is used in May on the coast of Kerry, and perhaps by crofters and islanders on other rocky shores, for cutting the kelp or seaweed harvest, which is then at its best for turning into manure.

In reaping corn, the reaper stoops to his work or kneels on one knee, and leaning forward grasps in his left hand the straw near the ground, pushes the blade of the sickle round it and draws it towards him, pushing his left hand over it at the same time, to avoid the cut. After each cut he raises his left hand to clear the ears from those of the next handful to be reaped; and when he can hold no more he lays out the bunch to his side, lifting it high over the standing corn with the ears supported in the curve of his sickle. As he works across the field he clears a strip about six feet wide (or less perhaps if the crop is heavy), reaping across the end of the strip from the outside to the inside and laying out his handfuls together in sheaves, ready for the binder.

A woman or girl generally does the binding. She must first shake out all grass and weeds from the straw and then, pulling out a handful from the bottom of the sheaf, she first twists it below the heads, turning it over so that they are held against the sheaf under the twist; and then dividing the bond she passes the two ends of it round the sheaf, again twisting them together and pushing them tightly under the bond. This, at any rate, is a common way of binding sheaves, but there are other sheaf-knots.

Towards the end of the day the reapers put down their sickles and assist the binders in setting up the sheaves to dry in stooks or shocks. One binder is sufficient for three reapers, sometimes for more; and it used to be customary in some places for the children also to follow the reapers, making 'lock-bonds' and laying the sheaves in them ready to be tied.

Nowadays reaping with sickles is almost entirely confined to small holdings, or small farms in districts which are full of large immovable stones, which make the use of machines impracticable. In such places two or three reapers, or a labourer and his family, are as many as will be seen working together; but when the sickle was the only means of harvesting all the corn that was grown, the farmer who had a large crop had to employ as many reapers as possible, in order to get the work finished before the corn was over-ripe. Where labour was cheap, the work was sometimes done with surprising speed. An old farmer in Ireland remembered seeing a wheat-field of fifty-five acres, in which no fewer than forty men were reaping with sickles, and women binding. On his going to look at the work, which was being beautifully done, he found two of the women fighting tooth and nail, tearing out one another's hair; the owner of the field was for letting them fight it out, but being a man of authority he intervened and stopped the battle.

In different districts there were various ways of arranging for the reaping to be done, and in some places it was customary for a band of harvesters to consist of a fixed number of men. In Northumberland six reapers were called a 'bandwin'; in Yorkshire three shearers went out with one binder and the four were spoken of as a 'yan'; but these terms are long since obsolete. In Cambridgeshire reapers worked in twos, the first making a lock-bond and laying in half the 'shoof', the second filling it and tying it. The leader was generally called the lord or headman. In some counties it was his duty to call the others up by blowing a horn in the morning, and he would blow it again as a signal to cease work for meals and at the end of the day. In parts of Essex the custom of sounding the harvest-horn was kept up till 1914.

Sometimes the harvesters worked in families, and the farmer would then apportion each family's work by tying a knot at intervals in the standing corn.

The Irish reapers cut the straw close by the ground, and

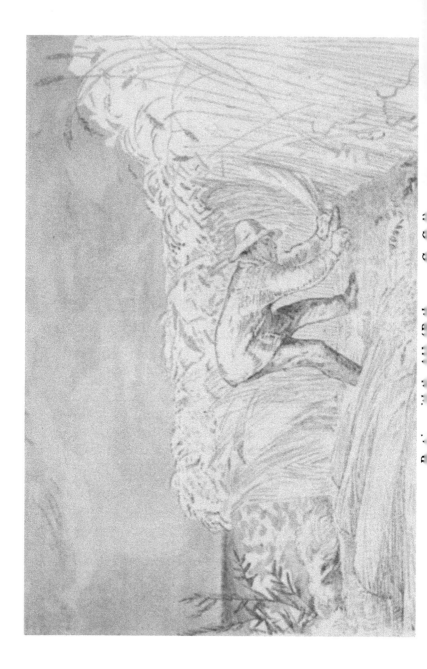

very little is wasted. This, though a slow process, leaves the field very neat and tidy; the ground is untrampled, the sheaves free from weeds and the straw straight and unbroken for the thatcher's use. But in England the stubble was left eight or ten inches long; and later in the year it was burnt to manure the land or 'hammered off' with a scythe to use as litter for cattle. In Essex the stubble was generally left till after Christmas as cover for the partridges; then it was cut off and used for making lambing-pens or for fuel.

A skilful and laborious man may reap a half-acre in a day. Formerly men worked for long hours throughout the harvest; and there are labourers still working in Somerset and Gloucestershire who have many times been up all night reaping by moonlight. One of them affirms that he and another man between them in one season mowed and reaped, of hay and corn, not less than two hundred acres of land. To sustain them in their Herculean labours a vast deal of fuel was needed. A gallon of cider to each man, and often ale in addition, was the regular daily allowance while this work lasted. The drink was carried in a wooden bottle like a little tub, slung at the belt; with a cork and an air stop which had to be removed before drinking from it. Every morning these were filled up by the farmer's wife and stood in a row outside the kitchen, one for each man. A farm near Bishop's Lydeard still continues the custom; perhaps others do also, but the farm labourer of to-day drinks very much less than his forefathers, for his work is no longer so constant and severe as to make it necessary.

Many farmers gave their men a meat dinner once a week, sometimes twice. The other meals during harvest were breakfast, elevenses, dinner and fourses—in some places elevenses was called 'beaver' or 'cheesing'—but there was a good deal of difference in the local significations of these terms and the times at which the meals were eaten. Meals at harvesting were generally somewhat different from those at other times. The school children had a holiday at harvest-time; in Norfolk the girls went out 'carrying elevenses' and 'carrying fourses', and the boys, whose duty it was to lead the horses which drew the harvest-waggons were said to be busied in 'hollering holdyer'; this was a signal to the men on top of the load to hold tight when the waggon moved on, and was yelled so loudly as to be heard, if possible, not only in the next parish, but in the next county too!

In different counties there were many ways of setting up shocks or stooks to dry before they were ready to carry to the stack or the barn. In wet districts, as soon as may be, the stooks are put into larger heaps called 'mows', the better to protect the corn from the wet.

The number of sheaves in the shock varies in different districts; formerly it was regularly fixed, but nowadays the terms 'shock' or 'stook' are loosely used by most farmers, and probably not many harvesters trouble themselves in the least about how many sheaves they set up, beyond the fact that too few are liable to be blown down, and too many will not dry easily. The stooks are made in straight lines down the field; the harvester holding a couple of sheaves by the heads, one under each arm, and dropping their butts on the ground at either side of his feet: so that the two rest upright against one another. More pairs of sheaves are generally added behind and before, so that the finished stook contains six, eight, ten or even twelve sheaves. It is a mistake to place an odd sheaf at the end, for this prevents the air from circulating through the corn and drying it. Formerly a 'shock' was generally understood to contain six sheaves and a 'stook', 'stowk' or 'hattock', twelve sheaves; in the northern counties (Derbyshire, Yorkshire, Cheshire, and Westmorland), twenty-four sheaves, that is, four shocks or two stooks, made up a 'threave', which was a convenient measure in those districts. In Cumberland, however, ten sheaves were reckoned to a hattock, or twelve to a stook. The term 'threave', 'thrave' or 'trace' was a pretty general one in several of the southern counties also, though it has now dropped out of common use. Where the land was ploughed in ten-foot stitches in Essex, the sheaves were set up in every alternate furrow, so that the rows of stooks, or 'traves' as they were called, stood at the breadth of two ridges apart from one another.

In the south-western counties, except Cornwall, stooks were made to contain ten sheaves, originally, it is said, for convenience in paying tithes when they were collected in kind; hence they are sometimes called 'tethins' or 'teddings'. The collecting of tithes in kind was commuted for money payment by Act of Parliament in 1826, and it is somewhat startling to find that it may still be no further off than a second-hand tradition. Last haymaking season an old Wiltshire labourer, who is still hard at work at eighty-four, beguiled the dinner-hour by telling stories which he had heard when a boy from an old man with whom he then worked. This man had explained to him how at harvest-time it had been his duty to carry round green boughs and lay one on every tenth stook, which was thus set apart for the parson. The farmer first carried his own sheaves, then the rector's waggon would follow and pick up all his, carrying them off to the tithe barn. This old labourer had several stories about tithing, always at the expense of the parson. A certain very mean and grasping rector called on one of his parishioners, a poor widow with a large family, having heard that her sow had farrowed and intending to claim the tenth pig of the litter. For some time she argued the point, but he was firm and not to be put to shame. At last she said, 'Well zur, if you do have the tenth pig then you do take the tenth child too, for I've got eleven o' they!' Whether the rector agreed to these terms is not related. The same parson had an argument with another of his parishioners on the subject of bees, claiming the tenth swarm of the season. In the end the bee-keeper entered his study one day with a skep in his hand, turned it upside down and shook out all the bees, exclaiming, 'Here you be sir, the bees is yourn and the hive's mine!' He made good his retreat before the rector could collect his wits, let alone the bees.

In harvesting other crops than wheat, different methods had sometimes to be employed. When barley was bound in sheaves, on account of the shortness of its straw, it had to be tied with double or lock-bonds, the binder fastening two small handfuls together by the ears and tying the tails the other side. In Essex and parts of Norfolk, and elsewhere, it was not bound at all, but being mown with scythe and cradle, was laid out in rows; and when the sun had been on these for some time, they were turned over with long three-pronged pitchforks, called barley-forks, so that the other sides should be dried also, and then carried loose in the waggon. It was a good plan, despite its seeming awkwardness, for barley is more easily injured by rain at harvest than any other crop, and it dries much more quickly loose than in sheaves.

In Kent barley used to be made into mows, and this was called 'haling'. Four sheaves were placed together two against two, their ears all together and butts outward, then four more on these with their butts somewhat off the ground; a third tier likewise, and finally three sheaves fastened together, with ears downwards so as to make a covering over the top. Thus the whole mow contained fifteen sheaves. Something much like this is done in Cardiganshire, where the stooks consist of four sheaves only. The mows are made by setting about fifteen more sheaves round a stook, their butts also on the ground; then another fifteen (or perhaps fewer) in a second and third tier; lastly three of four sheaves are tied close together at the top to keep out the wet. In Pembrokeshire wheat is sometimes thus made into mows, but not oats. In Co. Galway, where a good deal of reaping is done with sickles and the sheaves are very small, they are laid into 'barts', which contain thirty sheaves of wheat or twenty of oats. In other parts of the country, on account of the frequent rains at harvesting-time, the stooks are often made into mows as soon as the corn is dry enough to allow this.

Farmers used to leave their corn longer to dry in stooks than they commonly do now. Sometimes the reaping took a month, and when the corn was all stooked and finished— it might be on a Wednesday or Thursday—they would take another day or so to lay the rick foundations; and then on Saturday the farmer would very likely give his men a holiday and not begin stacking till Monday. But now corn may be cut, stacked, threshed and sent to the mill, all in a fortnight.

There were several old customs at harvesting, some local, others widespread, but all more or less of a ritualistic nature. In Devonshire, before a field was reaped, the farmer's wife was known to step in, before she would allow the reapers to begin, and cut the first few handfuls with her own hand, 'for the church'; these she would afterwards make into little sheaves and lay upon the altar. This was perhaps a pretty fancy of her own; but the other customs were possibly of pagan origin and had to do with the last sheaves cut. One of these was the bringing in of the 'neck', which was made of the last handful cut, the man who cut it standing between two sickles laid edge to edge on the ground crying 'I have a neck!' There were sometimes set responses from the other reapers and in the end a race to take it into the barn. The last load to be brought in, called the 'horkey load', was the centre of great rejoicing; it was crowned with a green bough and sometimes with a 'harvest-home sheaf' of great size, and the men, women and children rode home on it shouting and cheering. The great sheaf had to go at the bottom or in the middle of the rick and the bough was sometimes set on the top.

In Essex they went round to the farm or manor and 'hollered largess', which the master gave them in kind; one giving a barrel of beer or cider, another giving meat or bacon, and so on. In some places they levied contributions from the shopkeepers of the nearest market-town or hamlet. Then they would join forces and have the horkey or harvest-supper, it might be in a public-house, but more often in a barn. This giving of largess was gradually replaced by gifts of money, and in some places the harvest-supper was paid for by the farmer, especially if he were a well-to-do man. This was of course besides the two or three meat dinners a week which many farmers gave their harvesters. At the horkeys a few old songs, and probably more new ones, were sung, and in former years one or two old men would perform country-dances on a board. But since the passing of the Agricultural Wages Bill, the horkey has been generally abandoned, though one or two landowners in the eastern counties are still generous enough to give a supper each year.

T. HENNELL, *Change in the Farm* (1934)

XV

GLEANING

By T. HENNELL

FROM time immemorial the poorer people had a right
to glean in the harvest fields after the farmer had
carried his sheaves, and by this means many families
managed to keep themselves in bread throughout the winter.
The custom survives in a very few parts of the country; ten
or fifteen years ago it was much more common, but from
several causes it is quickly becoming extinct. The chief
reason is that there is no longer an urgent necessity for
it; the labourer's wages are higher, it is no longer common
for him to be in actual want, and so there is much less
incentive to thrift. With the increase of his pay he has
forfeited or relinquished his right to many of the perquisites which he had traditionally assumed for centuries
in the past. There is also a very strong kind of pride—
false pride perhaps—or a sense of social position, which
deters many from claiming rights which are theirs by in-
heritance; and when some give them up, the rest soon
follow for fear of being thought paupers. Besides, gleaning
was work for the women and girls, and 'you can't go gleaning in silk stockings!' But the introduction of reaping
machines is the chief reason why there are no gleaners
now. Reaping with fagging-hooks and scythes left more
for the gleaners, if anything, than did sickles; but the earlier
reaping machines and horse-rakes left less behind them, the
side-delivery reaper and the self-binder successively less
and less, till there was not enough to be worth the toil of
gleaning, and so the custom entirely died out.

After the field was raked one of the church bells was rung, at about eight in the morning and again at six in the evening, as a signal to the gleaners that they might be in the fields between those hours; and the women and children were up early and would wait by the gate till the bell was rung. In 1910 the gleaning bell was still rung in twenty or thirty parishes in Essex; in 1931, though there is still a little gleaning in several parishes, this old custom survives only at Farnham in Essex. A man was chosen to ring the bell and his name posted on the church door; each family of gleaners paid him a fee of twopence or sixpence for his services.

A stook or thrave of corn, called the 'guard-sheaf', was left near the gate until the farmer was ready to admit the gleaners; when it was removed they might enter and begin work. In Norfolk three sheaves, set up together and known as the 'policeman', answered the same purpose; in Lincolnshire there was a contrary custom of setting a white flag in the stubble as a signal that the gleaners might enter. People who were known to be honest and respectable had sometimes, by favour of the farmer, the privilege of gleaning between the thraves; much as Ruth had in the fields of Boaz. But before the majority could enter the stubble was handraked by men and boys, and these rakings made into little sheaves and put with the thraves. After these were carted the ground on which they had stood was likewise raked for the farmer, and even then the gleaners found more than they would find after the machine now. Where the parish boundary crossed a field, there was sometimes no little dissension between the gleaners of the two parishes. Each family reckoned to gather so many handfuls a day, if possible, before they went home. Sometimes they had a use for the straw, but more often they cut it off about six inches below the ears and left it in the field. They carried home the gleanings in large head-bundles, or in sacks or perambulators.

What little gleanings are gathered now, mostly between Saffron Walden, Dunmow and Braintree, are used to feed chickens; the old windmills which ground the corn and dressed the flour being done away with, and little or no bread baked at home.

An Essex labourer described how a man who had a hand-threshing machine used to thresh out the corn for them at night, but sometimes, it would be beaten out at home with flails. A miller, Metson of Sible Hedingham, used to grind the gleaners' corn, but it was necessary to wait for a wind. The usual arrangement was that he kept the bran as payment for the trouble of grinding, the cost of grinding and dressing being alternatively eightpence a bushel. The miller, to avoid confusion, numbered each family's gleanings in a separate bag.

The mother of each family used to bake once a week in the summer and once a fortnight in winter; and the bread, though rather dark, was better after ten days than white baker's-bread after two. Sometimes she would be up early and make 'apple-cake' or 'huffers' for the children's breakfast.

At that time every labourer's cottage had its own oven, and the wheat stubble or 'harme' was often the men's perquisite after the shooting season. The farmer lent his cart for carrying it, and it was made into stacks for heating the baking ovens. being pulled out from the stack with a 'harme-hook', or barbed spear, such as is still used in Wales. Though wages were low, there were in most

districts after-perquisites which made it possible for a
family to get enough food and fuel to live within their
earnings. The rent for a cottage might be only ninepence
or a shilling a week, milk threepence a quart, butter ten-
pence a pound; cider, cabbages and white turnips (where the
farms produced them) were often given for nothing.

T. HENNELL, *Change in the Farm* (1934)

XVI

HOPS

By GEORGE STURT

ON the north side of Farnham Street, where now are
building estates, with avenues and curbed footpaths
and so on, there was in my childhood one long succession—
two miles or so, from Coxbridge in the west to Bells
Bottom and Hale Church in the east—of hop-grounds.
('*Grounds*', notice. We thought it the mark of a contemp-
tibly ignorant stranger to talk of Hop-gardens.) Several
of these grounds had notable names—The Hart Ground for
instance. Others were familiar to us with purely local
names—Waterman's, Beaver's, Ford's. At what early age
I first heard of White-bines and Green-bines, and Kentish
Goldens (or Goldings, perhaps) I do not know; or how soon
it seemed important to note the degrees of fertility indicated
by the different length of poles—eighteen foots, twelve
foots, ten foots. I knew, early, that newly planted hops
needed only short slender sticks, usually 'spile'—or tops
of spoiled poles fit only for firing. It was not every year
that parsimonious growers would afford new poles; yet
every autumn they probably suffered grievously when old
poles, too brittle to bear the weight of clusters of hops all
but ripe, snapped before some untimely gale and let their
precious burden draggle into the muddy soil, or whip to
and fro in the wet wind. If this last happened—if the very
bine got broken so that its crop withered into brown flimsy
bunches called 'fliers'—it might be a serious loss, for a
pole might easily carry ten or twenty shillings' worth of

hops. So, several times I went with my father through his little ground, to see what havoc last night's wind had wrought, and to look on respectfully while he did what repairs he could with string. My little boots would grow heavy with sticky mud at such times.

Of the actual cultivation of hops I knew very little. Always some digging was going on: hop-ground work, I learnt afterwards, employed many an able labourer all the year round; and it was a disgrace to a grower to have weeds in his hop-ground. When a man had dug his 'task', he began again. The day was yet far off before any more permanent structure replaced poles for the hops to climb on. Poles had to be put up every spring—three, or else four to a 'hill'; and very early (as soon as the growth had fairly started) women went out 'tying'. The women carried little low stools, and, regardless of weather, sat down patiently to tie every uprising shoot to its pole, so that it might get a good start. Raffia had not been discovered perhaps, or more likely was beyond the women's means. Every tyer brought her own rushes for the purpose; which had been trodden into lissomeness on the cottage floor—as I discovered years afterwards in Bettesworth's cottage, when old Lucy Bettesworth was planning to go out 'tying' by and by. It was usually judged that the hops were growing fast enough, if they were 'half-way up the poles by midsummer'.

Then began anxieties in Farnham. Were the hops coming into bloom properly? Were they at all 'lousy'? Was there any sign of 'blight', or 'mould', or 'mildew', or 'red-spider'? Were the nights warm enough? Was there too much wind? Towards September old ramshackle carts full of 'gypsies' with sunburnt and unkempt children, and old sacks, and all sorts of odds and ends—dogs, cats, fowls—came making their leisurely way along the ancient street to this or that hop-ground, days before the picking was due to begin; and those were the days when there might be theft and when timid town dwellers were a little afraid of 'tramps' in country places, when as yet the 'hoppers' had not begun earning and had time to risk 'spoiling their hopping' by some mischief or other. This word 'hopping' should be noted, by the way. We never spoke of hop-picking.

Hopping was the season for school holidays in Farnham: a season of blowsy careless open-air life—not too comfortable, yet always enjoyable, with just a touch of excitement in it. It was shabby, jolly; it gave you an appetite. You wore old clothes and might go dirty; and on the whole it was golden and warm September weather—easy-going sunburnt autumn weather. To be sure, 'Hopping mornings' was a phrase with especial meaning in Farnham: it seemed to fit exactly the early hours, just after sunrise in September, while the air was chilly from the night and fingers ached, and a touch of frost made you wish for breakfast and something hot to drink. The really bad weather for hopping was steady rain, when pickers stayed away altogether, though hundreds would generally draggle into the hop-ground of a morning—say at about half-past six—in hopes that the weather would clear soon. As a rule, however, I remember hopping as a quiet and glowing time, warm, a little fatigued. September could even be too fine—too hot. In this case pickers would sometimes make a screen for themselves of poles already 'picked', to shade their 'standings' from too wearisome a spell of sunshine, when you stood hour after hour, picking hops into a basket.

And, even with that screen, hot sun could be really harmful. A properly ripe hop,* fit to pick, was firm and stiff between the fingers and heavy with yellow-golden dust—and helped to fill the basket: but in hot weather the hops were limp—'wilty' as we said—and did not soon enough make up a bushel.

And it was by the bushel that the picking of hops was paid for. Pickers who were out to earn money—and many Farnham folk took their annual holiday that way—would 'take a frame', that is to say engage themselves to an owner of hops, to be responsible for picking into one of his seven-bushel baskets until the crop was harvested. Up the insides of the big long baskets black marks measured the bushels; and if the hops were 'wilty' it took too long to reach and pass one of these marks, and the pickers felt tired and stifled and cross. At such times a little boy could get plenty of testy words and sour looks by blundering carelessly against a basket. The contents would too easily shake down to show a smaller measure. When the basket was full enough—at least you hoped it might be full enough—you could make it look a little fuller still by plunging both arms in deep and 'lightening' the hops in it. Then you called out 'Tallyman'—and the grower's representative came with his book (no longer tallies, in my time) to enter what you had picked. He was likely to scrutinize the basketful rather carefully, lest there should be too many leaves in it. A certain sort of pickers, out to make money and working too fast, probably needed looking after. 'Scratchers' they were called by other pickers. The full basket was

* Such a hop, squarish in shape, and yellowish-green in colour, might be an inch and a half or two inches long. If, as sometimes happened, little leaflets grew out of it, it was called a 'King Hop'.

emptied into a 'sarplice'—a wide open bag of coarse brown sacking, skewered over a wooden 'frame' and hung conveniently near to a 'setting' of pickers. The sarplice ('sarplier' was its more correct name—but we lived near Farnham Castle, and may have thought 'sarplice' would sound better to the Bishop) would hold eighteen bushels or so and then could be skewered up and swung into a cart and taken to the kiln for drying.

It was a pleasant thing in the dusky autumn evenings to pass close in Farnham streets to a load of freshly picked hops. There were many such loads, and most fragrant they were! The very streets smelt of hops as the cart went lumbering along, and every load of bulging sarplices told to a native of the town what had been going on all round him. Truly to think now of the loaded waggons and carts is to recover weeks of strong rough open-air autumn. Those plump earth-coloured, yet greenish, sacks, lying a-tumble all across the cart, meant so much. To see them was to see, and smell, the picturesque dismantling of a hop-ground— to hear the day-long chatter as of a flock of depredating birds; to catch the frequent laugh, the garrulous squabble, the rustle of the bines, the squalling of children. 'Tallyman' has been mentioned; oftener still sounded the cry 'Pole-puller'—for every ground had one or two men (I remember one went by the name of 'Ginger') whose duty was to keep the pickers supplied with 'poles', while of course he was responsible to the grower for due care of the plant. With a strong pocket-knife he cut all the bines of a pole twelve inches or so above the soil; with an ingenious implement called a Hop-dog he lifted the leaf-covered poles up out of the ground; and so he laid them down beside the 'frame' they had been allotted to, ready for the pickers to pick up and place over the basket for themselves, as soon as they were ready to gather the crop. (By the way, though the hops grew in bunches, and often a big bunch was torn whole from the bine, the hops had to be separated from it and put into the basket one by one.) I do not remember pole-pullers as individual men; but a memory of showy colour comes to me, soon resolved into sun-tanned skin, hairs shining curly on strong arms, hop-growth and sky; and, on the ground, a pile of men's things—white 'slops', yellow straw baskets, a black leather strap or so, a glass bottle with tea showing through it, a dark brown wooden beer-bottle shaped like a tiny barrel. Corduroy trousers and red cotton handkerchiefs add to the gaudy colour effect.

All day long the picking goes on; women scold at their children, who will neither work nor be still. 'Let me catch you, you young ninter, I'll gi'e you the bine!' (the bine being hop-bine, tough and twisty, like thin rope—a handy whip). So, for hours, the pickers stand—scolding, laughing, chattering, calling; until at last, between five and six o'clock, the cry goes across the ground 'No more poles!' For in fact enough hops have now been got to keep the kiln going until morning. So, as the poles already 'pulled' are finished, the tallyman makes his last round for the day, the sarplices are skewered up and carried to the cart (this is the pole-puller's job, horses being in fact too heavy to travel promiscuously over soil that must always be kept light) and meanwhile the fagged pickers gather together their things and straggle away in little groups or in families.

A spectacle in itself for an hour or two in the autumn evening—from before sunset until dark—was this piecemeal home-going of the Farnham 'hoppers'. Not that they went, all of them, home every night. There were many gangs of 'out-pickers'—families from far-away villages, or from the slums of Reading or of West London; and these came to stay until the hopping was over. Certainly it was one of the sights of the town to see some waggon-load of village folk arriving; or weeks later, to see the families going off again in their waggons, close packed; to see, to hear them; for especially on the return journey (glad to be sitting down again and going home) the villagers wedged into their waggons would be singing all along the streets—probably having money in their pockets, or wearing new clothes, or new boots bought in Farnham town. The slum dwellers too had no home to go to. They had but 'barricks'—mere shelters with absolutely no sanitary conveniences; while many 'gyppoes'—many of 'the royal family'—had pitched their tents in the same hop-grounds where they worked all day. But besides all these there were hundreds from the villages near Farnham —fathers, mothers, children, and all—hundreds who had locked up their cottages and trudged in out of the country for the day's work, wet or fine; who every nightfall trudged back again their mile or two, tired, dirty, hungry.

I was not aware, then, that anybody saw anything sorrowful in these endless streams of shabby-looking people along all the country lanes at nightfall—the women pushing perambulators, the children too often squalling, many a boy or girl dragging a piece of 'spile'—a broken hop-pole—perhaps for cooking a supper. But after many years I did hear men like Bettesworth (as I never at any time heard their 'betters') speak compassionately of the women's weary days. Truly it must have been weary work

for many a cottage woman (though I have no doubt many
husbands helped), seeing that in the cottages, reached at
last, the beds wanted making, while there was some washing up to be done, no water without going to the well, no
tap, no fire or gas. But these things I did not know; and
I never thought of the hoppers' home-going as anything
but jolly. After a day amongst hops, and out of doors, they
were sure to sleep well; and they would not only be hungry;
they would have plenty of relishing food. There was no
doubt about that. If a 'hopping morning' was one sign of
the season, so, no less surely, was the smell every night
of herrings frying! 'Red herrings' ('sojers') were the
meal everywhere. Every street or lane rejoiced in the crisp
appetizing smell of their cooking. The night air was
fragrant with it.

Another scent, that hung about the whole neighbourhood (obviously coming from a bluish vapour that poured
thick from the kilns now and then)—a strong suffocating
smell, came from the brimstone burnt with the drying hops.
Though it made folk cough and was choking to asthmatic
wind-pipes, all Farnham stoutly held that this brimstone
burning was good for the town; fumigating it whole-
somely with sulphur fumes when all those dirty out-pickers
might be bringing in fearful infections from their slums.
While I could still stand this smell (in after years I could
not enter a kiln where hops were drying—it set me wheez-
ing at once) I liked to see the golden drops that rained down
from brimstone thrown on to the charcoal fire; better still
I liked the potatoes which could be baked (in their
jackets, of course) in the ashes under the glowing grates.
The only necessary ingredient was salt, which you took
with you screwed up in a bit of newspaper. Plates and

knives and forks were not needed, no one ever missed
them.

The pay for picking was from three-halfpence to fourpence a bushel, according as the crop hung thick on the
poles or needed finding, one hop at a time, under the leaves.
A tedious job it always seemed to me: I never, at one sitting,
exceeded a third of a bushel. In picking, the golden pollen
from the hop flowers made one's fingers slightly sticky;
while the juice stained them black; and (you found it when
you went to wash) the leaves stung the skin. In the usual
absence of pumice-stone I found the rough stone edge of
the sink would rub off the worst of the stain; but nothing
prevented my hands from smarting—no mottled soap or
anything—when I dipped them into the cold water in the
hand-bowl. While picking one would sometimes find
amongst the hops a 'lion'—the larva of a lady-bird—and
this lion was viewed with favour, as the alleged devourer
of 'green fly'. Once or twice also I found amongst the
leaves a 'hop-dog'*—the huge green caterpillar of, I am
told, the hawk moth.

Not only was the picking poorly paid; quite often the
picker worked for a day or so actually without knowing
what the rate of pay was to be! What could helpless women
and children do otherwise than take the best they could get?
Only, sometimes a grower over-reached himself; for after
all, his crop could not wait for ever, and he ran serious risk,
if he failed to make people willing to gather it for him. And
they knew it. So my memory holds a dim picture of a
'strike'—an old dingy and mean street, a grey morning,
and a little gang of people, shabby and with no order,

* The pole-puller's tool for levering up hop-poles was also a
'hop-dog'.

straggling along the street, on their way to the house or shop of the stingy grower. I think they carried tin cans and other instruments of 'rough-music'. I think too they took for emblems of discontent a black flag, and a penny loaf on the top of a hop-pole, and a red herring or 'sojer'. Yet this sort of thing after all was an exception. In another memory I see twilight falling on the long street of Farnham, where (in these old days) there is no wheel traffic unless, now and then, a load of 'sarplices' is being carried to a kiln; and the street is thronged—it is Saturday evening—with hoppers loafing from shop to shop, from public-house to public-house. They are sauntering, good-tempered, careless, shabby; one threads in and out through a street full of them.

In yet another memory I am, myself, in my grandfather's kitchen (by dim candle-light) while somebody bustles in and out of the pantry to draw beer and carry it into the adjoining sitting-room. For there my grandfather is 'paying-off' hoppers. The old man (I must have peeped in at him) is at his usual table, looking very alert and capable; and perhaps he needed to be severe, for in the kitchen, beside the tallow candle, my aunt (or my elder sister perhaps) speaks of some 'dreadful' man there—who may be seen, in another peep, to stand black-avised, scratching, furtive, unwashed, opposite my grandfather. But all is well where my grandfather is.

When the picking was over the hop-growers had by no means done. First they had to market their crop; and then to start again, getting their hop-ground cleared up and ready for another year.

The marketing of course was preceded by drying and bagging. The hop-dryer had special tools, notably a very large but light wooden spade for shifting the hops on the 'hair-cloth' in the kiln, on which they were spread over the fires to dry and take the required tint and smell from the brimstone fumes. When dried they were heaped up at the end of the kiln, to be ready for bagging.

This was on an upper floor. For the 'bag' (a very stiff and thick canvas, yet not too strong for so precious a load) was hung down through a hole in the floor, so that the hops could be easily shovelled into it. An 'engine' fixed above it to the woodwork of the kiln enabled the dryer to screw the hops down, until the 'pocket' of them was full. (From underneath the hop-pocket showed as a pale cylinder, tight and hard, reaching up through the ceiling.) A full pocket of hops had to be carefully weighed—scales for this purpose being kept in every kiln. It usually weighed about two and a half hundred-weight.

Once, perhaps oftener, I watched my father 'drawing a sample' from a pocket of hops—a job to fill any Farnham man with pride, and performed in a sort of religious silence. With what reverence one seam of the pocket was ripped open far enough for the sample-drawers (a special implement of shining steel blades and screws) to be properly thrust in! Imagine two or three grave men at this job, anxious, holding their breath. At last the sample is carefully lifted out—a solid brick of dried hops some three inches square by six or seven inches long—and is passed from hand to hand for criticism. Did it consist of hops not crumbled into dust? Was there a good proportion of golden pollen in it? Was it a bright green colour, without too many brown patches—a sign of belated picking? All being well the sample might mean a fortune for the anxious grower. Well or ill, it was carefully wrapped up in the best

brown paper that money could buy—shiny brown paper,
very stiff and tough; and this parcel (proudly carried under
the arm) was wound round and round in great lengths of
strong string. It was never tied up, for whenever you met
another hop-grower it had to be solemnly submitted to his
inspection.

Perhaps the string was more firmly knotted when the
owner of the sample at last took it with him to Weyhill
Fair. But of this I knew nothing; I did not even know that
many growers were accompanied to the Fair by their wives,
and that the visit was a sort of annual holiday. I dimly
remember waking one October morning dawn, and seeing
my father in the cold-looking dusk starting to catch a train
for Weyhill. He came back at night, presumably well
pleased, for he had toys for us children. But he never had
much to do with hops, and certainly never made his fortune
by his little dabblings in that gamble. I think he was always
at the mercy of growers on a larger scale, who picked and
dried for him when it suited their convenience.

After the hopping it was woman's work, paid by the
piece, to strip the poles where they lay in heaps just as the
pickers had left them. The bines tossed together into brown
heaps were carted away and stacked in ricks, for litter—
especially for pigs.

The poles (the spile having been sorted out from them)
were piled up into 'aisles', and looked like tents all across
the hop-ground. There they stood throughout the winter,
restoring to the ground a look of order. It was needed.
For indeed all was untidy and desolate when first the hops
were down. It seemed as if winter had come; and it was
a common remark that the cold had been let in upon Farnham town. Certainly the wide hop-ground everywhere

looked bleak and desolate. The soil had been trodden flat
by the pickers; here and there a solitary pole, left standing
for some reason, stood gaunt and naked to the weather.
Occasionally a rook would settle atop of the pole; or
occasionally a battered tin can would be put there. Yet the
untidy hop-grounds made a fine playground for boys; one
felt it a proud thing, too, to climb one of the hop-poles.

Soon, in the winter, a new set of smells began, cheerfully
endured, if not indeed approved, in the town. For the sake
of the hops we felt it right that the whole neighbourhood
should reek of trotters, of guano, or any nameless filth the
growers chose for manure.

Another thing too marked the winter. New poles, to
replace the spile, were carted into the hop-ground, and had
to be pointed there. I suppose this was for the hop-ground
man to do. With one hand the man held the pole down on
a block a little lower than his knee, with the other hand he
swung down on the pole a light axe. And the axe must
have been sharp, and the hand that swung it strong, for
five or six chops pointed the pole. I was too little to know
or care much about this work, though I liked very well to
see a man at it, so deft, so industrious. With his trousers
strapped or tied under the knees, and with a short pipe
in his mouth, the man almost always looked good-tempered.
Why not? It was probably not too well paid a job—piece-
work, and with the chips for a perquisite; but it was out-
o'-doors; and with every blow of the axe a gratified sensation would run up the man's arm—the sensation of a
touch from the outside world that is not one's self.

GEORGE STURT, *A Small Boy in the Sixties* (1927)

XVII

'BOTTLES' AND MOLE-CATCHING

By GEORGE BOURNE

A N enquiry how his sister-in-law was faring led to a talk about her two sons, of whom one is out of work. The other (a basket-maker, blind or crippled, I do not know which) lives at home, and has just got a lot of work come in. 'Mostly stock work', Bettesworth believed, 'for some London firm he knows of.' But besides this, he has a hundred stone jars from the brewery, to re-case with basket-work. The handles and bottoms are of cane, the rest 'only skeleton work, as they calls it'. Bettesworth always loved to know of technical things like this.

Odd it is, I suggested, how every trade has its own terms of speech. 'Yes, and its own tools too,' added Bettesworth; and with deep interest he spoke of the tools this basket-maker uses for splitting his canes, dividing them 'as fine!' And the tools are 'sharp as lancets; and every tool with a special name for it'.

This reminded me to repeat to Bettesworth a similar account which a friend of mine had lately given me, and will publish, it may be hoped, of the Norfolk art of making rush collars. 'Very nice smooth collars,' Bettesworth murmured appreciatively. But when I proceeded to tell how the art is likely to die, because the few men who understand it keep their methods secret, this stirred him. 'Same', he said, 'as them Jeffreys over there t'other side o' Moor-ways, what used to make these little wooden bottles you remembers seein'. They'd never let nobody see how 'twas

done. But I never heared tell of anybody else ever makin'
'em anywhere.'

Yes, I remember seeing these 'bottles', like tiny barrels,
slung at labouring men's backs when they trudged homewards, or lying with their clothes and baskets in the harvest
field or hop-garden. It was to the small bung-hole in the
side that the thirsty labourer used to put his mouth, leaning
back with the bottle above him. Whether the beer carried
well and kept cool in these diminutive barrels I do not
know; but certainly to the eye they had a rustic charm. So
I could agree with Bettesworth's praises: '*Purty* little
bottles they got to be at last—even with glass ends to 'em,
and white hoops. They used to boil 'em in a copper—
whether that was so's to bend the wood I dunno. Little
ones from a pint up to three pints.... I had a three-pint
one about somewheres, but I couldn't put my hand on 'n
when I turned out t'other day. Eighteenpence was the
price of a quart one—but they had iron hoops.... But they
wouldn't let nobody see how they made 'em.... There was
them blacksmiths over there, again—*they* wouldn't allow
nobody to see how they finished an axe-head.

'These Jeffreys never done nothing else but make these
bottles, and go mole-catchin'. Rare mole-catchers they
was: earnt some good money at it, too. But they had to
walk miles for it. You can understand, when the medders
was bein' laid up for grass they had to cover some ground,
to get all round in time. I've seen 'em come into a medder
loaded up with a great bundle o' traps: an' then they'd
begin puttin' in the rods—'cause they was allowed to cut
what rods they wanted for it, wherever they was workin',
and they knowed purty near where a mole 'd put his head
up. 'Twas so much a field they got, from the farmer. I

never knowed nobody else catch moles like they did, but they wouldn't show ye how they done it, or how they made their traps.

'There was a man name o' Murrell—Sonny Murrell we always used to call 'n—lived at Cashford. *He* was a very good mole-catcher. One time the moles started in down Culverley medders, right away from Old Mill to Culverley Mill—it looked as if they'd bin tippin' cart-loads o' rubbish all over the medders. I never see such a slaughter as that was, done by moles, in all my creepin's.' (I think 'creepin's' was the word Bettesworth used, but his voice had sunk very low just here, and I could as easily hear the clock as him.) 'But they sent for Sonny. He was a *clever* old cock, in moles; they had to be purty cute to get round 'n—some did, though; you'll see how they'll push round a trap—but after he'd bin there a fortnight you couldn't tell as there'd bin any moles at all.'

GEORGE BOURNE, *Memoirs of a Surrey Labourer* (1907)

PART TWO

XVIII

TIMBER

By GEORGE STURT

UNDER the plane (it is little used now) or under the
axe (it is all but obsolete) timber disclosed qualities
hardly to be found otherwise. My own eyes know because
my own hands have felt, but I cannot teach an outsider, the
difference between ash that is 'tough as whipcord', and ash
that is 'frow as a carrot', or 'doaty', or 'biscuity'. In oak,
in beech, these differences are equally plain, yet only to
those who have been initiated by practical work. These know
how 'green timber' (that is, timber with some sap left in
it, imperfectly 'seasoned') does not look like properly
dried timber, after planing. With axe or chisel or draw-
shave they learn to distinguish between the heart of a plank
and the 'sap'. And again, after years of attention, but no-
how else, timber-users can tell what 'shakes' are good and
what bad. For not all shakes, all natural splits, in seasoned
timber are injurious. On the contrary, it was an axiom in
my shop that good timber in drying was bound to 'open'
(care had to be taken to prevent it from opening too far) and
that timber must be bad, must have lost all its youthful
toughness, if the process of drying developed no shakes
in it.

A wheelwright had to be quite familiar with little truths
like these in buying his timber, and then not forget other

considerations. In my shop we bought trees 'in the round'
—as they lay in the wood or the hedgerow where they had
been felled or 'thrown'. And, immediately, the season of
throwing came into question. Some oak, cut down in the
dead of winter, was called 'winter-cut'. It dried into
excellent material, the sap almost as hard, though nothing
like so durable, as the heart. Winter-cut oak always had
the bark on it. And for this reason it was scarce, and
'spring-cut' was commoner, the bark having a high market-
value for tanning. Most oak therefore was thrown early in
spring, when the running of the sap allowed the bark to be
stripped off easily. A further advantage was that this
spring-cut oak lent itself so well to the craft of 'cleaving'
spokes and laths.

It followed that the expeditions to buy oak were always
in the late spring or the summer. The bark had been stripped
then—it stood in big brown stacks beside the shining
butter-coloured 'sticks' or butts of timber, where they lay
in the brambles and newly springing fern. The 'lop and
top'—the branches and twigs—had also been stacked, the
bigger branches into cordwood, good for fires, the smaller
—the twiggy boughs—into 'bavins' or 'sprays' such as
bakers want for their ovens or potters for their kilns. So,
the ground was clear enough for the wheelwright to
examine his trees, and to measure them if he bought. And
a delightful outing he had of it.

For his quest took him into sunny woodland solitudes,
amongst unusual things and with country men of a shy type
good to meet. It was while looking at some oak (near the
Hog's Back) that I first heard the word 'puckeridge', when
a startled bird flitted away into a shady thicket. 'Nasty
p'isonous birds', said the man with me. Another time, as I

The Ring-dog in use

pushed through some brambles in 'Alice Holt' and came to a patch of spurge (or it may have been a mist of blue-bells), the tall young forester who was showing me the oak-trees suddenly dropped forward his full length without bending; and when he stood up he had got a rabbit in his hands.

Other timber than oak (always, of whatever sort, felled in winter) invited the timber-buyer into the winter woods or along leafless hedgerows. It was in stodging from hedge to hedge across wet water-meadows in February to look at some ash that my father took the chill which started his last illness. Elm was rather a haphazard crop with us: it would keep so long in the round that the season of throwing was not much if at all regarded—though I have seen it 'perished' by its own sap imprisoned in the unopened log. With beech it is just the reverse. During the War vast quantities of beech were spoiled, in the prevailing ignorance when to throw it and open the timber. Spoiled, I mean, for old-fashioned wheelwright work, chiefly in axle-trees. For this purpose beech should be hard as bone, and should therefore be cut down in November (they used to say in my shop) and opened into quarters by Christmas.

Another matter the wheelwright buyer had to know about was the soil the timber grew on. Age-long tradition helped him here. I, for instance, knew from my father's telling, and he perhaps from his father's, that the best beech in the district came from such and such a quarter: that the very limbs from the elm in one park would yield good 'stocks' (hubs for wheels); and that in a certain luxuriant valley the beautiful-looking oaks had grown too fast and when opened were too shaky to be used. Yet I didn't know (and paid for not knowing) that on the clay, in one hollow of Alice Holt, the oak had a nasty trick of going 'foxy-hearted'. I bought a small 'parcel' of trees there. They looked well enough too in the yard until the winter, when the sawyers began to saw them open. But then—tree after tree, sound at the butt, began about two feet up to disclose the 'foxy' middle, the rusty-looking pith like rotten string or rope running far up. I don't think my father or grandfather would have bought timber from that hollow. They knew 'England' in a more intimate way.

One point further concerned the timber-buyer. The best of trees, thrown at the right time, was after all useless if it could not for any reason be hauled up on to timber-carriage, or swung under 'nib' or 'timber-bob' (the same thing), for bringing home to the saw-pit. So it behoved the wheelwright buyer to refuse if, as sometimes happened, a tree had fallen in an inaccessible place. In steep hanger, or over shelving stream-banks, it might be impossible to place the skids from ground to wheel-top for rolling the tree up on to the 'carriage'. Running-chains and horse-power availed nothing then. The tree must rot where it lay. A slighter difficulty was a very miry road. The broadest wheels were not always broad enough to save the heavily-laden timber-carriage from sinking inextricably into a very soft surface. If the buyer of the tree could wait for dry weather, well and good. But what if the sawyers should have finished for him and gone away while his trees were stuck in the mud? These things had to be considered.

When the bargain was settled it remained to measure the timber—a pleasant and interesting job. To get the string between tree and ground (I never found a 'tape' measure of any use) I had a 'needle' or 'sword'—a slender and curved rod of iron—to push under the tree. At its end the needle was forged into a small hook like a button hook, and the looped string was then easily drawn back and so the circumference of the tree was taken. From that, to the 'girt', allowing for the thickness of the bark, and then (with slide-rule) calculating how many cubic feet of timber the tree held, was child's play. I liked it well, clambering over the prone tree-stems, amongst foxgloves and ferns perhaps. To guess the 'misure' of a tree, before actually taking its 'misure'—that in itself was a game. And, afterwards, the timber-carter liked to be told what the 'meetins' were— what was the average size of the trees he was sending his horses out to bring home.

GEORGE STURT, *The Wheelwright's Shop* (1923)

XIX

A FOLK INDUSTRY

By GEORGE STURT

TO say that the business I started into in 1884 was old-
fashioned is to understate the case: it was a 'folk'
industry, carried on in a 'folk' method. And circumstances
made it perhaps more intensely so to me than it need have
been. My father might just possibly, though I don't
think he would, have shown me more modern aspects of
it; but within my first month he took ill of the illness he died
of five months later. Consequently I was left to pick up the
business as best I could from 'the men'. There were never
any 'hands' with us. Eight skilled workmen or apprentices,
eight friends of the family, put me up to all they could: and
since some of them had been born and trained in little old
country shops, while this of my father's was not much better,
the lore I got from them was of the country through and
through.

The objects of the work too were provincial. There was
no looking far afield for customers. Farmers rarely more
than five miles away; millers, brewers, a local grocer or
builder or timber-merchant or hop-grower—for such and
no others did the ancient shop still cater, as it had done for
nearly two centuries. And so we got curiously intimate
with the peculiar needs of the neighbourhood. In farm-
waggon or dung-cart, barley-roller, plough, water-barrel,
or what not, the dimensions we chose, the curves we
followed (and almost every piece of timber was curved)
were imposed upon us by the nature of the soil in this or

that farm, the gradient of this or that hill, the temper of this or that customer or his choice perhaps in horseflesh. The carters told us their needs. To satisfy the carter, we gave another half-inch of curve to the waggon-bottom, altered the hooks for harness on the shafts, hung the water-barrel an inch nearer to the horse or an inch farther away, according to requirements.

One important point, which it's true was not always important (for hard roads, for instance) but was sometimes very important indeed, was to make the wheels of waggon or dung-cart 'take the routs', as we said. A variant of this was to get the wheels of a waggon to 'follow', the hind wheels cutting the same ruts as the front. One inch of variation was allowed, no more. The track of new dung-cart or waggon might measure 5 ft. 10½ in. or 5 ft. 11½ in. 'over', that is, from outside to outside. A miry lane at a farm revealed to me the importance of keeping to this measurement. Two parallel ruts went all down the lane, deep as the hub of a cart wheel. Many carts, for many years perhaps, had followed there; and plainly the lane would be impassable for any cart or waggon with wheels too wide asunder or too narrow. So, the wheel-spaces were standardized.

This was but one of the endless details the complete wheelwright had to know all about. For the complete wheelwright, acquiring skill of eyes and hands to make a wheel, was good enough workman then for the job of building a waggon throughout and painting it too; and all this was expected of him. There was a tale (of another shop than mine) of an aged man who, having built and painted a waggon, set about 'writing' (lettering) the owner's name and address on the small name-board fixed to the off front

side. He managed all right until he came to the address,
'Swafham' or 'Swayle', but this word puzzled him. He
scratched his head, at last had to own himself baffled; and
appealed to his mate. 'Let's see, Gearge,' he said, 'blest
if I ain't forgot how you makes a Sway!'

Gearge showed him.

Truly there were mysteries enough, without the mystery
of 'writing', for an unlettered man. Even the mixing and
putting on of the paint called for experience. The first two
coats, of Venetian-red for the underworks and shafts and
'lid colour' (lead colour) for the 'body', prepared the way
for the putty, which couldn't be 'knocked-up' by instinct;
and then came the last coat, of red-lead for the wheels and
Prussian-blue for the body, to make all look smart and
showy.

Not any of this could be left wholly to an apprentice.
Apprentices, after a year or two, might be equal to making
and painting a wheelbarrow. But it was a painful process
with them learning the whole trade. Seven years was
thought not too long. After seven years, a young man,
newly 'out of his time', was held likely to pick up more of
his craft in the next twelve months than he had dreamt of
before. By then too he should have won the skill that came
from wounds. For it was a saying of my grandfather's that
nobody could learn to make a wheel without chopping his
knee half-a-dozen times.

There was nothing for it but practice and experience of
every difficulty. Reasoned science for us did not exist.
'Theirs not to reason why.' What we had to do was to live
up to the local wisdom of our kind; to follow the customs,
and work to the measurements, which had been tested and
corrected long before our time in every village shop all

across the country. A wheelwright's brain had to fit itself to this by dint of growing into it, just as his back had to fit into the suppleness needed on the saw-pit, or his hands into the movements that would plane a felloe 'true out o' wind'. Science? Our two-foot rules took us no nearer to exactness than the sixteenth of an inch: we used to make or adjust special gauges for the nicer work; but very soon a stage was reached when eye and hand were left to their own cleverness, with no guide to help them. So the work was more of an art—a very fascinating art—than a science; and in this art, as I say, the brain had its share. A good wheelwright knew by art but not by reasoning the proportion to keep between spokes and felloes; and so too a good smith knew how tight a two-and-a-half inch tyre should be made for a five-foot wheel and how tight for a four-foot, and so on. He felt it, in his bones. It was a perception with him. But there was no science in it; no reasoning. Every detail stood by itself, and had to be learnt either by trial and error or by tradition.

This was the case with all dimensions. I knew how to 'line out' a pair of shafts on a plank, and had in fact lined and helped saw on the saw-pit hundreds of them, years before I understood, thinking it over, why this method came right. So too it was years before I understood why a cart wheel needed a certain convexity although I had seen wheels fall to pieces for want of it. It was a detail most carefully attended to by the men in my shop; but I think none of them, any more than myself, could have explained why it had to be so.

Some things I never learnt at all, they being all but obsolete even in that primitive shop. To say nothing of square-tongued wheels—a mystery I still think of with some awe—there was the placing of the 'tines' in a wooden harrow that remained an unknown secret to me. The opportunities of investigating it had been too few when cast-iron harrows, ready-made, banished the whole subject from our attention. I just learnt how the harrow was put together to be hauled over the field by one corner; but the trick of mortising the teeth—the 'tines'—into it so that no two cut the same track—this was known to one elderly man but never to me. The same man also failed to teach me how to 'line out' a wooden axle. Indeed, he forgot it himself at last. So it happened that when an ancient dung-cart arrived, needing a wooden axle for its still serviceable wheels, nobody was quite sure how to mark out the axle on the bone-hard bit of beech that was found for it. It was then that my rather useless schooling came in handy for once. With a little geometry I was able to pencil out on the beech the outlines of an axle to serve (in its clumsier dimensions) the better-known purposes of iron. Yet I have no doubt that the elderly wheelwright's tradition would have been better, if only he could have remembered it.

GEORGE STURT, *The Wheelwright's Shop* (1923)

XX

THE FARM-WAGGON

By GEORGE STURT

LONG after this peaceful period, I was really pained at the sight of an old farm-waggon being trundled along with a load of bricks towards what had been a quiet country place on the Surrey and Hampshire border. It was bad enough for bricks to be going there at all—to desecrate some ancient heath or woodland or field. Too plainly Old England was passing away; villas were coming, the day of farm-waggons was done. Here was this stately implement forced, like the victim of an implacable conqueror, to carry the materials for its own undoing. No circumstance of tyranny was omitted. Ignominy was piled upon ignominy. I felt as if I were watching a slave subjected to insult and humiliation. It was not so much that bricks were out of place. True, the delicate lines of the waggon-timbers had been shaped for other uses—for hay or for corn-sheaves, or flour-sacks or roots—but waggons have been used for 'brick-cart' often enough, and no wrong done. But here the shame seemed emphasized by the tractor. Instead of quiet beautiful cart-horses, a little puffing steam-engine was hurrying this captive along, faster than ever farm-waggon was designed to go. The shafts had been removed —as when Samson was mutilated to serve the ends of his masters—and although I couldn't see it, I knew only too well how the timbers would be trembling and the axles fretting at the speed of this unwonted toil. I felt as if pain was being inflicted; as if some quiet old cottager had been captured by savages and was being driven to work on the public road.

Very likely it was silly to feel so keenly as I felt then for a dead thing, and yet—the truth is, farm-waggons had been adapted, through ages, so very closely to their own environment that, to understanding eyes, they really looked almost like living organisms. They were so exact. Just as a biologist may see, in any limpet, signs of the rocky shore, the smashing breakers, so the provincial wheelwright could hardly help reading, from the waggon-lines, tales of hay-making and upland fields, of hilly roads and lonely woods and noble horses, and so on. The age-long effort of Englishmen to fit themselves close and ever closer into England was betokened in my old farm-waggon; and this the little puffing steam-tractor seemed to flout.

But where begin to describe so efficient an organism, in which all the parts interacted until it is hard to say which was modified first, to meet which other? Was it to suit the horses or the ruts, the loading or the turning, that the front wheels had to have a diameter of about four feet? Or was there something in the average height of a carter, or in the skill of wheel-makers, that fixed these dimensions? One only knew that, by a wonderful compromise, all these points had been provided for in the country tradition of fore-wheels for a waggon. And so all through. Was it to suit these same wheels that the front of a waggon was slightly curved up, or was that done in consideration of the loads, and the circumstance merely taken advantage of for the wheels? I could not tell. I cannot tell. I only know that in these and a hundred details every well-built farm-waggon (of whatever variety) was like an organism, reflecting in every

Hereford waggon (Mathon, nr. Malvern)

curve and dimension some special need of its own country-side, or, perhaps, some special difficulty attending wheel-wrights with the local timber.

Already, indeed, when I entered the business, the heyday of waggon-building was over and that decline had set in from which the old craft is now wellnigh dead. In details the new wheels of 1884 were made more cheaply than of old: for the countryman was growing so commercial that he would not—perhaps could not—afford to have work done with a single eye to its effectiveness. So with the waggon-bottoms. Just before my time a change for the worse had been introduced. The floors were now cross-boarded, although the costlier long-boarding had been a more useful if not a stronger device. This, as I say, was giving way to something cheaper. The earlier adjustments, which in fact had given the beauty as of an organism, were being neglected. Yet this neglect did not, could not, spread far. For years the old country traditions of waggon-building continued to be faithfully followed. Details which might not be cheapened still achieved the superb adjust-ments, and waggons grew into beauty, not to please artists who gushed about them, but to satisfy carters and to suit the exigencies of field and crop and road.

Apart from the shafts (or 'sharps' as we often called them) a waggon, though it looked one and indivisible, was made up of three main parts. First, on the fore-wheels, was the fore-carriage. The hind-carriage, on the hind-wheels, came next, carrying a 'pole' (like a long arm) to hold on to the fore-carriage centrally so as to be drawn along obediently behind it.

With a special and simple apparatus these two 'carriages' could be, and often were, used without the third portion.

For, when put together, they made a sort of trundling framework, as high in front as behind, very useful for loading hop-poles for the Farnham hop-grounds. This was every way an advantage. The hop-poles packed better than they would have done had the third portion—'the body'—been on the waggon; further it was worth while, for the sake of the horses, to dispense with the weight of the body if possible, seeing that the complete waggon, empty, weighed eighteen hundredweight or so. I am talking of a 'three-ton waggon'—to carry three tons, that is.

The body, too often spoken of as the 'bed', had its head, tail, waist; it lay on pillows (we called them 'pillars') and bolsters. When, new-made, it was at last hoisted on to its wheels, we spoke of 'gettin' her on to her legs'—using the feminine gender, perhaps in allusion to the complexity of the structure. Two 'pins' held the body in its place; a 'round-pin', of $1\frac{1}{4}$ in. diameter or so, fixing the head down to the fore-carriage; and a tail-pin (about five-eighths of an inch) sufficing to keep the tail from jolting up off the hind-carriage.

On recalling it I find myself wondering that a waggon was ever got together at all in my shop and under my management. Without pulleys or sling, strong arms alone had to raise the body from the ground and secure it to its two carriages; moreover, there needed to be a boy inside, to plunge the round-pin down into its place just at the critical moment—namely, when the pole from the hind-carriage was inserted into the fore-carriage and the body too was lying atop of them all right. Fewer than four men —to shift the wheels and so on—could hardly have done the necessary lifting—body and boy and all; and, as I was too ignorant, there was for the first months at any rate nobody to take command. Yet this seems not to have mattered. Waggons were constantly being 'taken down' for painting or mending, and then being lifted up again; and, as I remember no quarrel or disagreement over this work, I gladly believe that the workmen themselves liked to get it done efficiently and that their own friendly good temper taught them how to pull and lift together. Certainly it was an occasion for gruff jokes. Good humour saw us through. In one case, the round-pin having got jammed, a sledge hammer was called for to knock it down; whereupon the puny apprentice inside said 'Shan't I knock it down with my fist?' It's strange, how well I remember his smile after all these years.

GEORGE STURT, *The Wheelwright's Shop* (1923)

The Old Post-mill at Brill

(The 'round-house' has been removed, so that the central post and 'trees' are visible.)

XXI

WIND-MILL REPAIRS

By WALTER ROSE

AT the time of my boyhood the old wind-mills of this district of Buckinghamshire were still in regular use, as they had been for centuries. This village had two, and many of the surrounding villages had one or more, so that, whatever way one might happen to look, the sails of one or other of them could be seen turning merrily to the wind.

Could there be a more picturesque reminder of old English life, or any feature in more perfect harmony with rural surroundings, than those venerable old wooden mills? Whether they stood on the far hill-tops—and I well remember some six miles away—or on a gentle rise in the valley, their place in the picture was always pleasing, often its centre of attraction.

I know of no greater triumph of ancient English carpentry than those old post-mills, so called because they were constructed to balance on a central stationary post, which therefore carried all their weight. A few of the mills round about here were of a more modern type known as tower-mills, with circular stone-built or brick-built structures, and tops that were turned by means of a revolving fantail at rear, that automatically kept the sails facing the wind. In some tower-mills iron was largely used in place of wood; and this type never seemed to me to possess the natural and native character that was so definite in the post-mill.

Several of each type were maintained in a state of repair by my father's men. Much of the work at wind-mills resembled that done at water-mills—the recogging of the wheels and the repairs to floors, spouts, bins and hoppers. All this was common to both types. But the post-mills, built of wood throughout, were subject to much more wear and tear than the tower-mills; the weather-boarding of their sides and roofs, the outside ladders and turning beams were always exposed to the elements and needed frequent repairs. But in both types the repair and renewal of the large wooden sails was by far the most important job. These sails were subject to much stress and strain from the buffeting wind, whether the mill was working or not, and often demanded our men's attention.

The work was interesting—as work always is when it deals with ancient structures. We had to follow the ancient methods of work, the methods of carpenters who had first planned and raised those ponderous structures: who had shaped that mighty central post, thirty inches square at base, out of a solid oak tree, and placed it there with the huge mill securely balanced on its top. This large central post never needed any attention, so well was it framed to the large cross-beams (called 'trees') on which it rested endwise. Often did I stand beneath those large beams to gaze above in awe and wonder at their colossal strength. There, in the dim light of the round house beneath the mill rose the large post and beams, securely braced together by strong curved oak stays, the post disappearing through the apex of the roof into the mill above.

I always felt that the service fulfilled by those beams, those strong stays and that large post, was worthy of oak, and I would reflect on their long years of silent growth in the forest. These reflections could least be escaped in the mill with which I was most familiar, a real giant, much larger than the normal post-mill. Its large cross-beams rested on brick piers that were incorporated in the walls of the round house. This raised the whole construction to a greater height and allowed for a longer length of sails, and consequently more regularity of movement. This mill was not so erratic in its speed as those smaller mills whose cross-beams were near the ground.

The sails always reached to about two feet from the ground, and it was an enthralling experience to stand before them—as I often did—when a stiff wind was blowing, and watch them go roaring by: to note the 'swoop', 'swoop' of each sail as it passed and to follow the orbit of one as it rose to almost sixty feet in the air, immediately to descend and swiftly pass again. The mill was near the school that I attended and we children learned to know the different degrees 'quarter', 'half', 'threequarter' or 'full sail', to which the miller reefed the sails according to the strength of the wind that was blowing. To us it savoured of the sea, and ships, about which we had often heard and read, but had never seen. We were always on good terms with the miller, who had sons about my own age with whom I was friendly. And so it happened that contact with these boys and the work that was done in my father's yard, made me familiar with the construction and working of the mills of the district.

Many times have I seen the men turn the body of the mill, adjusting its position to face the wind. The large turning beam projected from the side of the mill opposite the sails, on which side was also the entrance door and the large broad step ladder that led to it. A large wheel, probably taken from an old farm cart, was fixed to the end of the turning beam, supporting it from the ground. It had

travelled round and round the mill so many times, that a
permanent circular rut was formed where it went. This
mill was far too heavy to be turned by man power alone;
therefore, at the end of the turning beam, a windlass was
fixed, and just outside the circular rut a series of dwarf oak
stakes were fixed in the ground. To the stakes the miller
would attach a chain from the windlass, and so by turning
the handle he could bring the mill into the right way of the
wind. There was always a vane on the top of the mill to
which he would look to know the exact position. We boys
liked to be in the mill when it was being turned; sometimes
there was a groaning sound from the top of the central post,
which carried all the weight and on which it turned. The
top of this post reached to the second floor of the mill, in
which a large cross-beam was incorporated, having a hole
in the centre that fitted a pivot on top of the post: this
formed the axis on which the whole mill revolved and to
this cross-beam all the mill was framed. While the mill was
being turned, the foot of the outside ladder was lifted and
attached to the turning beam by a short chain.

But to go into the mill when it was working to a full
strong wind was a never-to-be-forgotten experience, for
only in that way could its true character be understood and
appreciated. To climb the broad oak ladder and go in through
the doorway was to enter into the very pulsation of its life.
There one was conscious of movement, above, beneath and
around: a quivering of the whole structure, a continuous
creaking and rumbling, a sensation of terrific power swaying the whole framework. For the moment the knowledge
of the large sails outside was forgotten, giving place to the
feeling that the whole structure was in the grip of some
unseen power: force wrestling with force.

White clinging dust was everywhere. The crooks and crannies of the mill were many, but all were utilized for some purpose and all were smothered with dust. It covered the floors and clung to the walls and ceiling, which was the underside of the wooden floor above. It clung to the slippery step ladders that led from floor to floor; the miller was white from head to foot, but he did not mind it. To us it seemed to be his native element. Only on the top storey, just under the boarded roof, where the air was crisp and sweet, was there freedom from dust. Here were the hoppers into which the grain was poured, also a roller and chain that drew up the full sacks from the round house; and the large axle to which the huge sails outside were fixed. On the axle just inside the mill and close to the boarded wall, was a large wooden wheel with wooden cogs and a curved brake, also of wood, on its outside rim. This brake could be operated by a rope that passed through the wall of the mill, and was used by the miller to bring the sails down one by one when he was reefing them. In a sudden gale this brake was sometimes insufficient to bring the mill to a full stop and the miller had to wait for a lull before he could do so. But when he left the mill every night, in addition to lowering the circular brake he was careful also to chain the wheel, lower the stones, and reduce the sail-cloth in order to keep the sails from moving. No one knew what gale might arise in a night, and it was very risky not to leave the mill safely secured. When I was a boy another mill in this village for some reason unknown broke loose in a gale one night. The friction of the wooden brake, or the action of the stones grinding together without corn between them, produced fire, and before it was discovered the mill was in flames. It was burned to the ground. This happened just after my father's men had thoroughly repaired it. It was just after harvest and the mill was full of gleaners' corn waiting to be ground. In its place a tower-mill was built, with an iron roof and modern machinery.

The old large wooden mill had two sets of stones, one for grinding meals for cattle and the other for grinding wheat flour for men. Its period of real prosperity was before my time, when the village was self-sustaining and the villagers lived on the corn they had grown themselves. In still earlier days, before the enclosure, many more held small strips of land, and almost all baked their own bread in the brick ovens within the ingle-nooks of the old fire-places. To them the mill was a prime necessity of daily life, and a continued lack of wind was a serious matter for the whole neighbourhood. I am glad that for many years of my life the old mill continued its service, although by that time the flour trade had almost forsaken it. It was fascinating to stand by the bins on the lower floor and watch the warm meal pouring from the spout that led from the revolving stones above; and from thence to climb the step ladder that led to the second floor and pause for a moment to look through a small porthole at the surrounding country —the peaceful fields of the valley, each separated with neat hedgerows, where men and teams of horses laboured, cultivating the land. And as one looked the vista would be cleft every few seconds by a huge sail that swept close by. It was a vivid reminder that they were turning outside, and that they and the winds constituted the motive power of the mill.

The sails were made in my father's yard—they were much too large for the workshop. Unlike all other work executed by our men, they were made 'on the twist', so

The Tower-mill at Lacey Green, Bucks.

that when in position the extremity was flat to the wind, but the 'heel', or end nearest the centre, presented a splayed face. I asked why they were not made evenly splayed all along the sail and was told that a splay at the far end would gather up the wind behind and retard the speed. It may have been correct: I knew well enough that our men simply made them as they had been made before, according to a system that experience had proved the best.

The four sails were always made of strong yellow deal slats crossed and nailed together; the cross-slats being framed into a shaft of pitch-pine. It was to these slats that the miller tied the sail-cloths, reefing them according to the strength of the wind. The four sails were bolted to two large oak stocks, each about twenty-eight feet long, by about fourteen inches square at the centre. The stocks were sawn at our pit to fit the large iron cross-eyes. These projected from the mill, and were part of the large iron axle that passed into the top storey, where it was connected with the large wooden axle off which all the machinery was propelled. It was a big undertaking to fit sails to a mill. My father would travel many miles to find suitable butts of oak of the right length and size to cut for the stocks. I remember that when they arrived on the timber carriage we had difficulty in turning it into the yard, so long were they. And after they were sawn to size, the centres to fit the eyes and each end tapered to less measurement, there remained the more formidable task of getting them into position.

For this purpose my father kept a crab windlass and block pulleys. The axle was over thirty feet from the ground. It was by no means easy to pass the stocks into it. The power of a man at the top of a forty-round ladder is limited, but it was at that position that Jesse Saw manoeuvred them into the eyes; other men below manipulating the ropes and pulleys. When the first new stock was drawn sufficiently far upward through an eye, the position of the axle was reversed, which caused the stock to sink downward, until it finally rested on a shoulder that had been shaped for the purpose. Wedges of wood were then driven all round until the stock was rigid in the eye, after which a fillet was spiked at the side of the eye corresponding to the shoulder.

The stocks securely fixed, our men would proceed to fix the sails to them, a job equally difficult. Those familiar with the peculiar construction of a wind-mill will know that the sails are not vertical to its face, but are at an angle inclining toward the mill at top. Why this is so I have never been able to ascertain. Was it that the old builders found that the line of the wind was on an incline downward, or was it that it was more favourable to the balance of the mill that the sails should pitch back at top? Our men could not answer that query, but they well knew that it caused much more trouble in getting the sails into the exact position (on the slope) and in holding them there while Jesse Saw, on a ladder, bored the holes, with an auger, to take the iron bolts with which the sails were secured to the stocks. When the first sail was securely fixed, it was necessary to turn it upwards and hold it there for the fixing of the opposite sail. This was no easy task with no sail to counterbalance it. When two sails only were renewed—and there were never less—the old sails were available to pull at, but when all four were renewed it needed much levering, at the inside wheels and pulling at the blank end of the stock, to get the first sail upwards. Sometimes the work was done

in cold weather when it was a bitter experience to stand
and hold on to a rope without any exercise. The work was
dangerous, as was all the other exterior work of the mill—
the repairs to the outside boarding of the walls and roof—
but I never remember an accident to our men when
engaged in it. I am glad that it was so, and glad to know
that it was my father's men who last repaired the old mills
of this district, before they disappeared from the landscape
for ever.

WALTER ROSE, *The Carpenter's Shop* (1937)

PART THREE

XXII

STRAW

By T. HENNELL

TILL lately wheat-straw was an important product of farms in Bedfordshire and Hertfordshire on account of the straw hat trade centred at Luton. The straw is exceptionally fine and bright in this district, nearly white in colour and, when steamed and pressed, with a beautiful natural polish. When the wheat was reaped with hooks, the stubble was left eight inches or a foot long and so only the finest part of the straw was kept. Later when reaping machines were used, a coarser plait was introduced, made from the thick straw near the ground.

The straw was drawn by hand, a labourer standing astride three sheaves of wheat and pulling it out in handfuls by the ears. These were cut off and separately threshed, and the clean reed was sold in bundles of eighty pounds. The straws were cut into slips or lengths close by the joints and graded according to fineness, different grades being used for the various patterns of plait. Before use the straws were sometimes dyed and split into threes, fives or sevens by 'machines': small hand tools with a sharp point and several radiating blades or fins. Having been steamed and bleached, they were passed through mills or rollers to prevent them from breaking and were then worked into plait.

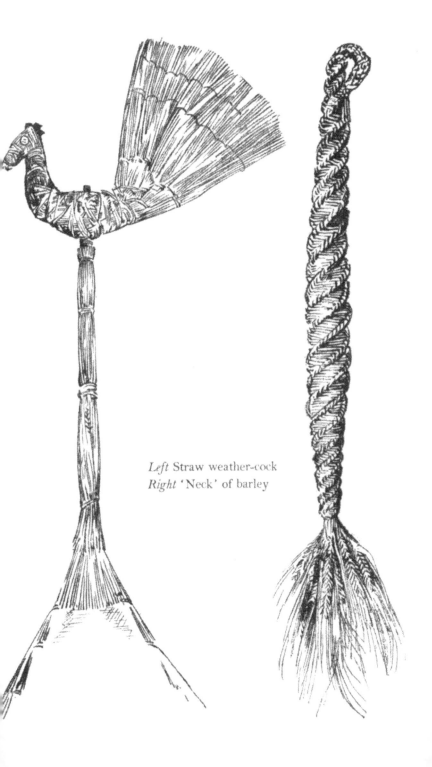

Left Straw weather-cock
Right 'Neck' of barley

The commonest sort was made by boys and children and paid for at the rate of fivepence a score (twenty yards). It was quite usual for children to be made to plait a score between coming out of school and going to play. For troublesome and elaborate plaits women were often paid half a crown or three shillings a score and so were able to earn eighteen shillings a week, while their husbands got only sixteen shillings a week as labourers. They had to buy the straw which they used, but this was not a heavy proportion of the cost. Thirty yards of fine plait or twenty-six of coarser quality went to make a hat. No doubt it is a craft which could well be revived with much advantage to many British farmers and cottagers, but it has been almost killed by Japanese plaits and coarse rye-straw imported from France.

These two letters from the Hertfordshire woman who made the plaits which are here illustrated are so much better than anything else I can say about this graceful rural art that they may be added without apology.

Sir,

I am sending you the patterns of Plait that you ask for trusting they will be what you want and as you would like them to be but I want you to take in to consideration that it is quite 30 Years since I have done any but the Rustic for after the death of my Parents I went out to Service for some years as Cook and Cookhousekeeper and Workinghousekeeper and when I come home the only sort going was the Rustic but I know how to do it but when one goes from 4 to 11 it does seem as if one cant get along but all that one wants is patients and I am like my Parents I always see my work done in my own mind before I begin and I don't think their is much to complain about but with more practise more perfection my Cousins house where you went to ask

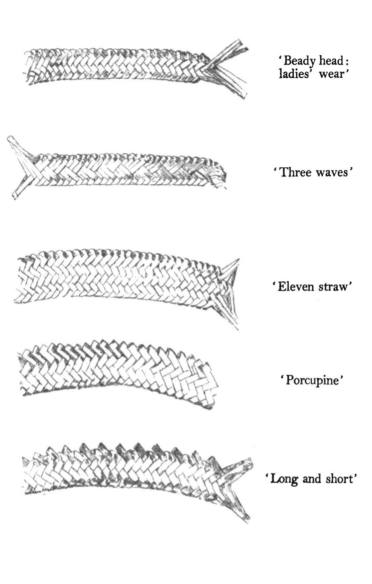

'Beady head:
ladies' wear'

'Three waves'

'Eleven straw'

'Porcupine'

'Long and short'

'Rustic, No. 1'

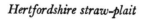

Hertfordshire straw-plait

if I lived their she is quite taken with the three Wave and now I think that is all I have to say hoping it is not so cold where you are as it is here now as to the cost of my time I dont think if I say 2s. and postage you can think it to much it aint the time it takes to do the Patterns but the time it takes to get ones fingers to a certain form as all are different make of work and the hand has to get a different form of movement.

Yours Faithfully,
E— F—

I am sorry that I did not know that Mr Davis had retired from farming but did not tell you about him to make a stupid of you all I knew was what Mr Jeffs told me and I cant say how long it is ago for time flies so fast one is not always awear of its speed.

The reply to my letter with the money:

Sir,

I have know doubt by this time you are beginning to think my a very carless sort of a person in keeping you so long with out an answear to your letter I received on Monday morning but when I tell you the cause you will understand and yow know we have had a very sharp spell of cold weather and Gardening was put in the back grounds but when the longed for change came one had to put in all their time, and that with a will I have got my Beans, Peas, Carrots, and Parsnips in I was very pleased to hear that the Pattens where all that yow wished them to be and trusting that it may be the right work in the right place thanking you very much for the Order.

Yours Faithfully,
E— F—

T. HENNELL, Change in the Farm (1934)

XXIII

THE LACE-MAKERS

By H. E. BATES

THE Ouse and the Nene, dissimilar in so many things, are bound together, curiously enough, by an art which flourishes scarcely anywhere else in England. Since it is an art which was, in origins, and still is, in essence, foreign to England, it is all the more remarkable that these two valleys, one rural and one industrial, should have fostered it with equal distinction. All along the Ouse, from Buckinghamshire down through Bedfordshire and on into Huntingdonshire, and all down the Nene, on a parallel line, little old women, looking appropriately as if they had come out of Dutch paintings, are still faithfully devoted to this lovely art, the art of making lace on pillows. These women are almost all old and they are the last of their kind. They have a look of seeming to be immemorial, with their lace caps, white hair, Rembrandt faces and skinny yellow hands, whereas they are, in reality, not only dying themselves but devoted to a dying art. Their immemoriality is a myth. They will not endure, and unless something in the way of a small revolution happens, their art will flutter out like a candle with them. This loss to English rural arts will be much the same as if the writing of lyric poetry had died with Herrick. For of all English country arts this lace-making is indisputably the most delicate and fascinating.

There is a quality of mystery about it, and the lace itself is a miracle of beauty. There is no other art quite so simple-looking and artless and yet so intricate and miraculous, so apparently aimless and yet so faithful to a thousand rigid principles.

Lace-making holds its distinction of place for several reasons. First, it is not only an art but a history, and not only a history but also a romance and a tragedy. Secondly, it is surprisingly delicate and difficult, learned only by great patience and trial and perseverance and ingenuity. Thirdly, its products are superb; pillow lace stands in relation to the rest of rural crafts exactly where poetry stands in relation to the rest of literature; at its best it is pure lyricism. Finally, apart from other things, it is the only craft I know of which the tools themselves are also works of art and histories and, at their best, bits of lyricism too.

On top of all these eulogies, none of which is extravagant, it is ironical to have to confess that the art is not really English at all. It has been English for four hundred years, but its origins are Flemish and French. It would be remarkable, in fact, if such a delicate art were English in origin. It is altogether too dainty and fanciful; its intricacies are carried to rather too rare a point of art. What is greatly to the credit of the English nature, as personified by the people of the Nene and the Ouse, is the genius with which it adapted, nourished and even improved an art which was essentially foreign to it.

It's an ill wind, even a dictatorship, that blows no good, and it was virtually a dictatorship, in 1567, and another, in 1572, that brought lace-making to this country. In 1556 Philip II of Spain succeeded Charles V of Spain as ruler of the Low Countries, and a peaceful country became a bloody country. Philip, like all dictators, ancient or modern, royal or common, believed in the shedding of a little blood. And in 1567 there ensued what is now, with almost medical propriety, called a purge but what was then, more plainly, called a massacre. Those who escaped that occasion, about 100,000 in all, and, of course, Protestants, came to England, and they brought lace-making with them.

They drifted, for some not very clear reason, to Bedford-shire. In 1572, when that other and more famous purge occurred, the massacre of the Huguenots in France, the surviving lace-makers, mostly from Mechlin and Lille, drifted almost in the same direction, to Northamptonshire and Buckinghamshire. And those three counties are, still, except for a corner of Devonshire, the exclusive home of English pillow-lace.

Thus the history of lace-making is, from the first, drenched in blood. Later, much later, it was to be drenched in tears, not idle tears, or even very catastrophic tears, but the miserable tears of small children working very early and very late in dark Victorian lace-schools at pillows they were not big enough to lift. Later, too, I have no doubt that other tears fell, the tears of old women forced to sell the most beautiful lace in the world to hucksters who squeezed them down to a last damnable farthing. One single bead of intricate Buckinghamshire point-ground lace takes hours of concentrated and expert work, yet I have seen such lace, three inches wide, for which the best huckster's price was eighteenpence a yard. No wonder its creator declared bitterly: 'I'll go into the damn fields and spud turnips afore I make another blessed stitch at that price.'

6-2

That same little woman, eighty-five years old and still giving lace lessons, suffers, though she does not know it, from claustrophobia, the fear of confined spaces. 'When I was a mite of five I went to lace-school. One day I was too unwell to do my pattern. I said I couldn't do it. The teacher said: "You'll do it or you shall be locked in the barn." And now if you were to lock me in a room I should go mad! I've suffered for it all my life.'

Yet without that early training and bitter concentration her art would never have been so fine. Lace-making is not learned in five minutes, and it is best learnt by the very young. Jesuits and lace-teachers had one thing in common: they took their pupils early and what they taught was never forgotten. If they taught by cruelty one can only point, in consolation and even vindication, to the results. The process of making lace on a pillow is difficult to describe, let alone to learn. It is one of those arts that look charming and simple, but which is, in reality, intricately difficult.

First, anyway, there is the pillow. Sausage shaped, looking rather like a soldier's kit-bag, it is stuffed with straw—with, if you please, a truss of straw, a truss being half a hundredweight. That straw is hammered and beaten down with a hammer until the pillow is like a pillow of iron.

The pillow stands on a wooden rest, a sort of trestle, waist high. Then, over the curve of the pillow, goes the parchment. On the parchment is the pattern, pricked out with pins, and sometimes also with ink.

After that the processes are, to the lay mind, nothing but mysterious. You may watch a lace-maker until your eyes drop out, but if you do not know you do not know, and there it is. You will see the bone and wooden bobbins and their cottons flick and rattle in and out of place, and you will see the flash of pins moved and marshalled in order to make the stitches, but that, roughly, is as much as you ever will see. The bobbins move so rapidly that their manipulations seem like the jingling and rattling of someone gone quite crazy.

Those bobbins, next to the lace itself, are the supreme attraction of the art. They are, as I say, the only tools of any art that I know which are themselves works of art.

They fall, roughly, into two types: the bone and the wooden. An average bobbin is simply a piece of bone or wood, crudely or intricately carved, about three or four inches long. It looks like a miniature stair balustrade. On the bottom end of it is wired a ringlet of beads, a spangle. It will contain from one to nine beads: turquoise and rose and milk and plum and amber, some as big as and very like robins' eggs, some no bigger than peas. All are delightful. There are, occasionally, special spangles. There is a bird-cage spangle: a single large bead contained in a cage of tiny beads of rainbow colours. There was, once, a famous spangle of a single enormous bead called Kitty Fisher's Eye, named after the actress.

But it is the bobbins themselves that are really pieces of history. In the old days bobbins were either carved at home or bought from a travelling dealer. If they were home-made they were almost always wooden, delicately carved out of rosewood, maple, plum, apple, laburnum, yew, apricot, box, cherry, blackthorn, even ebony.

If they were bought they were, mostly, of bone. Now a bone bobbin, being white, will take a design in colours. Therefore it became the fashion not only to decorate bone bobbins but to inscribe them. When dealers came round to take orders for new bobbins they took orders for inscrip-

tions too. A baby had been born—inscribe its name on the
bobbin. Someone had been married—mark the occasion
and the date on the bobbin. Someone had died—let him
have a bobbin memorial.

And gradually this game of inscribing and decorating
bobbins grew to almost crazy proportions. Lace-makers
began to inscribe on their bobbins not only births and
deaths and marriages and betrothals, but sweet nonsense
and prayers, hopes and fears, verses and texts, puzzles and
songs, and, finally, murders and suicides.

When I first saw a murder bobbin I was shocked and
embarrassed. It commemorated, I felt, some awful event
in the family. Now I know better.

I cleared up the mystery by talking to two old Northamptonshire ladies, one nearly ninety and as hearty as a chicken,
the other younger but deaf.

'Oh! whenever there was a murder and the murderer was
hung in Bedford Gaol we had his name put on a bobbin,
that's all. Ain't that right, Miss Perkins?'

'Eh?'

'I say we had all the murderers put on bobbins, didn't
we? You come with me to see old Joseph Castle hung,
didn't you?'

'Eh?'

'I say you came to see old Joseph Castle hung at Bedford,
didn't you? You remember—up he went and then all of a
pop he was gone. It was fourpence to have a murderer put
on a bobbin,' she said to me.

The airy callousness of these old ladies was something
to think about. Later, I was able to buy a Joseph Castle
bobbin—'Joseph Castle, Hung 1860'—and to discover too,
that Castle came from Luton and murdered his wife. On

the March night when he was hanged the relatives of the murdered woman held a party. Every one who went to that party had a bobbin inscribed with Castle's name.

The variation of bobbin designs and inscriptions is immense. Inscriptions are done in scarlet, scarlet and black, black; vertically, horizontally, spiral-fashion. They record all manner of family and local histories, of personal hopes and loves and fears and tragedies and aspirations. They are endearing or silly or naughty or serious or nonsensical: Lovely Thomas; My Darling; Forget-me-Not; Dear George; Sweet William; I will for ever love the giver; Be ye Therefore Ready; Kiss me Quick; Dear Mother; Love me Truely; Love don't be Falce. Spelling is often crazy. There are scores of others: Kiss me Quick my Mome is coming; I love the Boys; Merry me Quick; I wonce loved them that ner loved me; My Hart Hakes for you; My Dear I love you as Birds love Cherries; Sarah Dazeley, Hung 1843. Sarah, who was beautiful and only twenty-two, was a sort of female Blue-beard, knowing that arsenic was the shortest way with husbands.

Just as, in fact, indifference is the shortest way with art. No art ever died of anything but indifference. Art thrives on opposition, even more than oppression, and it has even thrived on stupidity. But it has no response to indifference except death. And it is simply indifference which is killing the art of making lace on pillows, an art which had its heyday in an age which, for all artistic purposes, not to speak of others, we now despise.

All this is, of course, exactly typical of mankind. It is not so much true that familiarity breeds contempt as that it breeds indifference, and after almost four centuries of familiarity with lace-making it is now in the natural order

of things that there should be a breeding of indifference.
But wait. Give the whole business another ten or twenty
years, until the old ladies are mouldering in the church-
yards of Ouse and Nene and their precious bobbins and
bobbin-winders and parchments are kicking about in the
forgotten corners of antique shops, and indifference will
suddenly give way to a fashionable yearning to have it all
back again. This is one of mankind's oldest tricks: indifference to a thing while it possesses it, then a great howling
and crying out for it when the thing has gone. So with lace.
In fifty years, unless something remarkable happens, lace-
making on pillows will be a memory. Then, unless the girls
of that day go naked, which is, of course, very possible, a
great sighing and moaning will go up for the lovely work
of past days, of, in fact, our own generation.

   And Ouse and Nene will, incidentally, have lost the thing
which binds them together. It is odd to think of these two
rivers, so like threads of water themselves, being bound
together for almost four hundred years by threads which
were almost as miraculous and delicate as water itself. It
is absorbing to think of this metaphorical binding together
of two really separate peoples devoted to an art dropped
on their doorstep by another country. And, not least, of
their adaptation of it: their aspiration toward new designs,
the modelling of patterns on the things they loved, tulips
and roses and honeycomb and chains and the strange shapes
of spiders' webs and even the frost on Victorian window-
panes, and the inspired growth of the bobbins, reflecting
the crude genius of the people, recording their births and
deaths, tears and laughter, jealousy and silliness, in a way
that no other art has ever quite accomplished.

                              H. E. BATES, *Down the River* (1937)

A LIST OF COUNTRY INDUSTRIES
AND A LIST OF BOOKS

A COMPREHENSIVE study of Rural Economy, past and present, would have to deal in some detail with the following topics, though this is not an exhaustive list. The contents of this book are arranged in an order more or less corresponding; accounts of some typical aspects of the life and work of our countryside are given, but descriptions of certain better-known activities have been omitted to make room for others of special, if less common, interest.

The reader desirous of following up these and other rural themes should see particularly Hennell's *Change in the Farm*, the Rural Industries Bureau's *Reports, England's Green and Pleasant Land*, Bennett's *Problems of Village Life*, Orr's short *History of British Agriculture*, and the writings of George Sturt (Bourne), Adrian Bell and A. G. Street. It is hoped that the List of Books appended— most of them are still in print—will (*i*) provide for that further reading of complete works by authors here represented, which it is one of our main objects to encourage, and (*ii*) help to fill in the outlines of particular interests. It is, perhaps, hardly necessary to add that the volumes mentioned are not all recommended without critical reservation, or that List (ii) is merely suggestive.

I. AGRICULTURE

Village and Labouring Conditions.
Dairy Farming.
Carting: Horses.
Sheep Farming.
Stock and Poultry Farming.

Tillage: Hedging, Ditching, Drainage, Manuring, Ploughing, Sowing.

Haymaking: Stacking.

Harvesting: Rick-making, Threshing.

Cultivation of Root and other Crops.

Fruit-growing: Grafting, Pruning.

Minor Activities: Bee-keeping, Cider-making, Malting, Hop-, Flax-, Willow-, and Teazle-growing, Turf-cutting, Charcoal-burning, Mole-catching, etc.

II. CRAFTS ANCILLARY TO AGRICULTURE

Thatching.

Woodwork: Carpentry, Wheelwrighting, Cartwrighting.

Blacksmithing.

Saddlery.

Farm and Cottage Building.

Farm and Cottage Economy.

III. OTHER RURAL INDUSTRIES

Straw- and Rush-plaiting.

Basket-making.

Pottery.

Textiles: Lace-making.

Quilting.

Joinery: Cabinet-making, Garden Furniture-making, Bowl-turning and Spoon- and Ladle-making in Wood.

Underwood Industries: Hurdle-making.

Wrought Ironwork.

Lime-burning.

LIST OF BOOKS

(i) AUTHORS REPRESENTED IN THIS BOOK

Bates: *Old English Country Life*; Batsford.
    Down the River; Gollancz.

Bell: *Corduroy, Silver Ley, The Cherry Tree*; Cobden-Sanderson, 3 vols., or in 1 vol. (Novels).
    Folly Field; Cobden-Sanderson (Novel).
    The Balcony; Cobden-Sanderson (Novel).

Bell: *By-Road*; Cobden-Sanderson (Novel).
    The Shepherd's Farm; Cobden-Sanderson (Novel).
    Poems; Centaur Press.
(Bell): *The Open Air—An Anthology of English Country Life*; Faber.
    (The List of Books from which the extracts were taken
    forms an excellent bibliography of the subject.)
Cobbett: *Rural Rides*; Dent. (Edited by Edward Thomas.)
    The Progress of a Ploughboy; Faber. (Edited by William Reitzel.)
    Cottage Economy; Davies.
Hennell: *Change in the Farm*; Cambridge University Press. (Second
    edition has extra illustrations.)
Jefferies: *The Gamekeeper at Home*; Murray, Cape.
    Greene Ferne Farm; Smith Elder (Novel).
    The Amateur Poacher; Murray, Cape.
    Wild Life in a Southern County; Murray, Cape. (Edited by Beach-
        Thomas, and illustrated, Nelson.)
    Hodge and his Masters; Methuen. (Revised by Henry William-
        son.)
    Round About a Great Estate; Murray.
    Nature Near London; Chatto.
    Red Deer; Longmans.
    The Life of the Fields; Chatto.
    The Dewy Morn; Macmillan (Novel).
    The Open Air; Chatto.
    After London and *Amaryllis at the Fair*; Dent. (Two Novels
        in one volume.)
    Field and Hedgerow; Longmans.
    The Toilers of the Field; Longmans.
    The Hills and the Vale; Duckworth. (Edited by Edward Thomas.)
(There are books of Selections edited by Daglish (containing
        The Gamekeeper at Home, complete, Dent), Looker (Con-
        stable), Tickner (Longmans), and Williamson (Faber).
        The standard critical Biography is by Edward Thomas
        (Dent). See also a Review of Lives and Works by Q. D.
        Leavis (*Scrutiny*, March 1938, p. 435).)
(Jefferies): White's *Selborne*; Scott.
Rose: *The Carpenter's Shop*; Cambridge University Press.

Street: *Country Days*; Faber.
  The Endless Furrow; Faber (Novel).
  Farmer's Glory; Faber.
  The Gentleman of the Party; Faber (Novel).
  And England in his Heart; Faber (Novel).
  Hedge-Trimmings; Faber.
  Strawberry Roan; Faber (Novel).
  Already Walks Tomorrow; Faber (Novel).
  Thinking Aloud; Faber.
  Farming; Faber.
  Land Everlasting; Bodley Head.
  Farming England; Batsford.
  The Heart of England; British Heritage Series.
  Moonraking; Eyre and Spottiswoode.
  The Country Calendar; Eyre and Spottiswoode.
Sturt (Bourne): *The Bettesworth Book*; Duckworth.
  Memoirs of a Surrey Labourer; Duckworth.
  Lucy Bettesworth; Duckworth.
  William Smith, Potter and Farmer; Chatto.
  A Farmer's Life; Cape.
  Change in the Village; Duckworth.
  The Wheelwright's Shop; Cambridge University Press (complete
    or abridged).
  A Small Boy in the Sixties; Cambridge University Press.
  A Year's Exile (Unpublished Novel).
  The Ascending Effort; Constable (Æsthetics).

(ii) BOOKS FOR FURTHER READING

The Cambridge University Press publishes many Memoirs
containing valuable comment. Messrs Batsford's publications on rural topics are most useful; many of the books in
their list contain bibliographies, and the list should be
consulted: see particularly Ditchfield, Hartley, Jekyll,
Pulbrook, Quennell and Wickham. Lord Ernle's *English
Farming* contains (in Appendix I) a Select List of Agri-

cultural Writers down to 1700. The following may be specially noted: Palladius, Walter of Henley, Fitzherbert, Tusser, Markham, Hartlib, Blith, Evelyn, Houghton.

Abercrombie: *The Preservation of Rural England*; University of Liverpool Press.

Ackland: *Country Conditions*; Wishart.

Allan: *Farmer's Boy*; Methuen.

Anon.: *England's Green and Pleasant Land*; Cape.*

Ashley: *The Bread of Our Forefathers*; Oxford University Press.

Viscount Astor and B. S. Rowntree: *British Agriculture*; Longmans.

William Barnes: Poems.

Bayne-Powell: *English Country Life in the Eighteenth Century*; Murray.

Beach-Thomas: *Village England*; (MacLehose) Black.

 The Yeoman's England; (MacLehose) Black.

 The Happy Village; Benn.

E. N. Bennett: *Problems of Village Life*; Butterworth.

H. S. Bennett: *The Pastons and their England*; Cambridge University Press.

 Life on the English Manor; Cambridge University Press.

Robert Bloomfield: *Farmer's Boy* (Verse).

Blunden: *The Face of England*; Longmans.

Richard Bradley: *Survey of Ancient Husbandry and Gardening* (1725). *Complete Body of Husbandry* (1727).

James Caird: Writings on English Agriculture (*c*. 1850).

John Clare: Poems. (Complete, ed. Tibble (Dent); Selected, ed. Blunden.)

Clark: *Country Mixture*; Allan.

Claxton: *Agricultural History*; Macmillan.

Cook: *A Manor Through Four Centuries*; Oxford University Press.

Coulton: *Chaucer and his England*; Methuen.

 The Mediaeval Village; Cambridge University Press, and other Writings.

* Now published under its author's name: J. W. Robertson Scott (editor of *The Countryman*).

George Crabbe: Writings.

Cripps-Day: *The Manor Farm*. (Contains facsimiles of several old books of Husbandry.)

Curtler: *The Enclosure and Redistribution of our Land*; Oxford University Press.

Darton: *English Fabric*; Newnes.

Davies: *The Case of Labourers in Husbandry* (1795).

Ditchfield: *Old Village Life*; Methuen.

    The Cottages and the Village Life of Rural England.

Stephen Duck: Poems.

Eden: *The State of the Poor*; 3 vols. (1797).

Lord Ernle (R. E. Prothero): *English Farming—Past and Present*; Longmans.

Finn: *The English Heritage*; Heinemann.

Finch: *Life in Rural England*; Daniel.

Fisher: *Life and Work in England*; Arnold.

Fordham: *English Rural Life*; Allen and Unwin.

Garnier: *Annals of the British Peasantry*; Allen and Unwin.

Gibb: *A Farmer's Fifty Years in Lauderdale*; Oliver and Boyd.

Gibbs: *A Cotswold Village*; Murray.

Gonner: *Common Land and Enclosures*; Macmillan.

Grant: *Everyday Life in Old Scotland*; Allen and Unwin.

Hall: *Our Daily Bread*; Murray.

Hammond: *The Village Labourer*; Longmans.

Thomas Hardy: Novels; Macmillan.

Harris: *The Farmer's Life*; Dent (Prose and Verse Anthology).

Harrison: *A Description of Britain* (1577).

Hartley: *Here's England*; Rich and Cowan.

    Made in England; Methuen.

James Hogg: *The Shepherd's Calendar*.

Hoskyns: *Talpa—Chronicles of a Clay Farm*.

Howitt: *The Rural Life of England* (1838).

Hudson: *A Shepherd's Life*; Dent, and other Writings.

Hutchinson: *The Art of T. F. Powys*; *The Bookman*, January, February and August 1933. (Articles, including a complete bibliography to 1933.)

Jusserand: *English Wayfaring Life—Fourteenth Century*; Benn.
Kebbell: *The Agricultural Labourer*; Allen and Unwin.
Kendon: *The Small Years*; Cambridge University Press.
Nathaniel Kent: *Notes on the Agriculture of Norfolk* (1796).
    Hints to Gentlemen of Landed Property (1775).
Kenward: *The Roof Tree*; Oxford University Press.
Langland (ed. Skeat): *Piers the Plowman*; Oxford University Press.
(Skeat): *Pierce the Ploughmans Crede* (*c.* 1394) and *God Spede the Plough* (*c.* 1500); Oxford University Press. (Two Poems in one volume.)
Leavis and Thompson: *Culture and Environment*; Chatto.
Mairet: *Hand Weaving To-day*; Faber.
Marshall: *Agriculture in the Southern Counties* (1799), and other Writings.
Massingham: *Shepherd's Country*; Chapman and Hall.
    Country Relics; Cambridge (illustrated by Thomas Hennell).
    A Countryman's Journal; Chapman and Hall (illustrated by Thomas Hennell), and other Writings.
(Massingham): *English Country*; Wishart.
(McDonald): *Agricultural Writers from Sir Walter of Henley to Arthur Young—1200 to 1800*. (Exhaustive bibliography.)
McNeillie: *Wigtown Ploughman*.
Millin: *The Village Problem*; Allen and Unwin.
Mitford: *Our Village*; Dent.
Morris: *The Village College*; Cambridge University Press.
Newbigin: *Tillers of the Ground*; Macmillan.
Orr: *A Short History of British Agriculture*; Oxford University Press.
Orwin: *The Open Fields*; Oxford University Press. (An account of the famous Laxton Fields in Nottinghamshire.)
    The Future of Farming; Oxford University Press.
O'Sullivan: *Twenty Years A-Growing*; Chatto.
Peake: *The English Village*; Benn.
Porteous: *Farmer's Creed*; Harrap.
T. F. Powys: Novels; Chatto.
Riches: *Eighteenth-Century Agriculture in the County of Norfolk*.
Rider-Haggard: *A Farmer's Year*; Longmans.

Rider-Haggard: *Rural England*; Longmans, 2 vols.

(Robertson-Scott): *The Countryman*; A Quarterly Review of Rural Life and Industry.

D. H. Robinson: *The New Farming*; Nelson.

Maude Robinson: *A South Down Farm in the Sixties*; Dent.

Rogers: *Six Centuries of Work and Wages*.
    Agriculture and Prices in England—1259 to 1793; Oxford University Press, 7 vols.

Thomas Ruggles: *A History of the Poor* (1793).

Rural Industries Bureau: Publications.

Russell: *The Farm and the Nation*.

Rynne: *Green Fields—A Journal of Irish Country Life*; Macmillan.

Sackville-West: *The Land*; Hogarth (Verse).

Sassoon: *Memoirs of a Fox-Hunting Man*; Faber.

Scott: *The English Countryside*; Ward (Photographs).

Seebohm: *The English Village Community*; Cambridge University Press.

Cecil Sharp: Writings on Folk Music; Novello.

Slater: *The English Peasantry and the Enclosure of the Common Fields*.

Adam Smith: *The Wealth of Nations* (1776).

Somerville: *The Whistler at the Plough* (1842–7).

Stapledon: *The Land—Now and Tomorrow*; Faber.

Stevenson: *Crafty Smiths*.
    The Din of a Smithy; Chapman and Hall, or Cambridge University Press (abridged).

Edward Thomas: *Collected Poems*; Faber.
    Prose Writings.

F. G. Thomas: *The Changing Village*; Nelson.

Torr: *Small Talk at Wreyland*; Cambridge University Press, 3 vols., or in 1 vol. (abridged).

Trotter: *Seventeenth-Century Life in the Country Parish*; Cambridge University Press.

Jethro Tull: *Horse-Hoeing Husbandry* (1733; edited by Cobbett in 1822).

Thomas Tusser: *500 Points of Good Husbandry* (1580), and other Writings.

(Various): *Rural Industries of England and Wales*; Oxford University Press, 4 vols.

Virgil: *Georgics* (Verse).

Warlock: *The English Ayre*; Oxford University Press, and other Writings on Old English Music.

Warren: *A Cotswold Year*; Bles.

Watson: *The Common Earth*; Dent.
   English Country; Cape.

J. A. S. Watson: *Rural Britain Today and Tomorrow*; Oliver and Boyd.
   The Farming Year; Longmans.

J. A. S. Watson and Hobbs: *Great Farmers*; Selwyn and Blount.

Williams: *A Wiltshire Village*; Duckworth.

Wills: *Shepherds of Sussex*; Skeffington.

Viscountess Wolseley: *The Countryman's Log-Book*.

Wood: *A Sussex Farmer*; Cape.

Wordsworth: *Lyrical Ballads* (1798) and *Poems* (1807); Oxford University Press.

Arthur Young: Tours, Travels, etc. (1770–1809).

Defries: *Sheep and Turnips—Being the Life and Times of Arthur Young*; Methuen.

There is much valuable incidental comment in the works of such writers as Izaak Walton, Gilbert White and George Borrow.

C.G.H.

GLOSSARY

Many technical terms are sufficiently explained by the contexts in which they appear. Only those about which there is a possibility of doubt are included here.

ARABLE (n., adj.). Capable of being ploughed; fit for tillage.

AXLE-TREE. Fixed bar, on the rounded ends of which the opposite wheels of the cart revolve.

BAST. Flexible, fibrous bark cut into strips.

BAVIN. Brush- or firewood.

BINE. The climbing hop stem.

BLOCK PULLEYS. System of pulleys mounted in a frame, used in lifting great weights.

BOBBIN. Small cylinder, round which the thread is wound to be easily wound off again.

BOBBIN-WINDER. Contrivance for winding thread on a bobbin.

BUTT. (i) Blunt end, bent over, of a bundle of thatch. (ii) Trunk of a tree from ground to branches.

COUCH. Species of grass with long creeping root-stalks.

CRAB WINDLASS. Portable machine, consisting of a frame with a horizontal barrel on which a chain or rope is wound by means of handles and gearing.

CRANK. The angle where the blade of a scythe becomes narrower, towards the handle.

CROFTER. One who rents and cultivates a small piece of arable land attached to a house.

DIP (n.). Candle made by dipping a wick into melted tallow.

FELLOES (pron. 'fellies'). Curved pieces of wood which, joined together, form the rim of a wheel.

FILLET (n.). Narrow strip of wood fastened to a surface to serve as a support, or to strengthen the angle formed by two surfaces in wind-mill repairs.

FOGGER. Farm-hand chiefly engaged in feeding cattle.

GONFALON. The Standard of some Italian republics, often with streamers, hung from a cross-bar.

GRUB-AXE. Used in grubbing up roots and stumps.

HOPPER. Receiver like an inverted pyramid or cone, through which grain for grinding passes into a mill.

NIBS. The two short handles projecting from the shaft of a scythe.

PIN (n.). Piece of tapering wood hammered in to join parts of a waggon.

POMONA. Roman goddess of fruit-trees.

POPPAEA. Wife of Nero.

'PUMMY' or POMACE. Mass of crushed apples in the process of making cider, after or before the juice is pressed out.

RAFFIA. Soft fibre from the leaves of a certain palm, used for tying up plants, and for plaiting or weaving into baskets.

REAL ESTATE. Immovable property in lands or houses.

REEF (v.). To shorten a sail by taking in a part and securing it.

RENNET. Mass of curdled milk used in making cheese.

SEDGE. Various coarse rush-like plants growing in wet places, used in thatching.

SLIP (n.). Small plant, or tree-shoot taken for grafting.

SPANGLE (n.). Decoration of beads on a bobbin.

SPUD. A spade-like implement with a narrow chisel-shaped blade, used for digging or weeding.

SPURGE. Plant which has an acrid, milky juice possessing medicinal properties.

SQUARE-TONGUES. Tenons cut at the end of spokes, for mortising into the felloes.

STOCK (n.). The hub of a wheel or wind-mill sails' support.

STOCK-JOBBING. The implication is, of course, of rash or dishonest speculation in stocks and shares—a practice naturally abhorrent to a man like Cobbett.

SWEEP (n.). Plate or frame for sweeping off grain.

TALLY (n.). Simple mode of keeping record of an amount or account. May be a piece of wood on which notches are made.

TINES. The projecting sharp points on a harrow or other tool.

TUMBRIL. Cart so constructed that the body tilts backward to empty out the load.

WINNOW. To expose grain to a current of air so that the chaff is blown away.

CAMBRIDGE: PRINTED BY
W. LEWIS, M.A.
AT THE UNIVERSITY PRESS